WHAT DO I KNOW
about my God?

MARDI COLLIER

WHAT DO I KNOW
about my God?

MARDI COLLIER

journeyforth®

Greenville, South Carolina

Library of Congress Cataloging-in-Publication Data

Collier, Mardi, 1949-
  What do I know about my God? / Mardi Collier.
    p. cm.
  Summary: "A Bible study showing how knowing God should affect a believer's thinking and daily life"—Provided by publisher.
  ISBN 1-59166-681-3 (perfect bound pbk. : alk. paper)
  1. God—Biblical teaching. 2. God—Study and teaching. I. Title.

BT103.C655 2006
231—dc22

2006004812

Cover Photo Credits: Hutchinson Photography (sheep), Unusual Films (author)

All Scripture is quoted from the Authorized King James Version.

What Do I Know About My God?

Design by Rita Golden
Composition by Melissa Matos

© 2006 by BJU Press
Greenville, South Carolina 29614
JourneyForth Books is a division of BJU Press

Printed in the United States of America
All rights reserved

ISBN 978-1-59166-681-3

15 14 13 12 11 10 9 8 7 6 5

To Ken, my "favorite!"
You have been my best example of the love
and kindness of Jesus.

To my children, Matt, Evan, Aaron, and Natalie,
and my added children, Kelly, Natalie Sue, and Naomi:
you make me smile in my heart!
I love you and learn from you.

Table of Contents

PART 2: HOW KNOWING GOD IS CHANGING MY THINKING

Acknowledgments

I first of all want to thank my best friend and husband, Ken, who has had more impact on me spiritually than anyone else I know. When he was in college, he was greatly influenced by the Bible passages that present Christ as a servant, and he has attempted to make that his way of life. He truly does have a great love for and desire to please God, and he tries to live his life for others. I am often rebuked by his patience and kindness towards people, especially me. He has been my cheerleader and advisor in this effort.

I want to thank THE WILDS for so kindly lending their help, expertise, and resources in getting this project started.

This book would not have been possible without all of the gifted secretaries, proofreaders, and editors who cheerfully spent many hours correcting my grammar, sentence structure, punctuation, awkward phrases, and anything else that needed fixing. Thank you to Julie Herbster, Karen Cleary, and Cheryl Reid for their time and very helpful suggestions. Suzette Jordan has been a wonderful and patient editor and her expertise has been invaluable.

I want to say an especially *huge* thank you to my friend Caroline Floyd, who believed in this project and invested much time and energy in typing, proofing, editing, researching, and nursing it along. I am extremely grateful and know that God will reward her for her labor of love!

PART ONE
Knowing God

ABOUT *My God*

Hi! My name is Mardi Collier. I'm nobody special—just an ordinary, very average person who has been discovering that God is extraordinary. I want to share my testimony of a simple, life-changing devotional idea that has helped me in my quest to know God.

Do you have a desire to know God? I know I do. At THE WILDS Christian Camp, where my husband Ken and I have worked for many years, I have been exposed to a number of godly men and women who issued the challenge to know God. I certainly wanted to, but I wasn't sure how to go about it or even where to begin. Ken suggested that I start by going through the book of **Psalms**, finding out whatever I could about the character of God. The result has been an ongoing study about God that has changed my thinking and my life! I feel totally inadequate to teach anyone else about our wonderful and mighty God, but at the same time, I am so grateful for what He is teaching me about Himself through His Word that I want to tell everyone.

What I would like to do in this little book is to explain the study and then share some examples of how the truths I am learning about my God are affecting my life. Since I am new at this, I will express my thoughts simply and practically, as if I were writing a letter to a friend. Because this study has made such a big difference in my Christian walk, it is my sincere and heartfelt desire that it will help others grow in their relationship with God too.

As you read, I would like to ask you to please pay special attention to the Bible verses. We tend to skim over the verses when we're reading a book, but it's what God says and Who God is that matters. In **Hebrews 4:12** God says, *"For the word of God is quick, and powerful, and sharper than any twoedged sword, piercing even to the dividing asunder of soul and spirit, and of the joints and marrow, and is a discerner of the thoughts and intents of the heart."* It is only God's Word that can pierce and change our hearts and lives.

Why Do I
Need to Know God?

BECAUSE GOD WANTS US TO KNOW HIM

Our God wants us to know Him and His Son Jesus. Did you realize that? We tend to think of God as big and awesome and far away, and it is definitely true that we will never fully know or comprehend Him. **Romans 11:33–34** says, "*O the depth of the riches both of the wisdom and knowledge of God! how unsearchable are his judgments, and his ways past finding out! For who hath known the mind of the Lord? or who hath been his counsellor?*"

How can our finite minds ever fathom such an almighty and awesome God? It's not possible. But what is exciting is that we can learn and know what He has revealed to us about Himself and His Son in His Word. Any Christian can know that much about God, and He wants us to.

> **Deuteronomy 4:29** *But if from thence thou shalt seek the* LORD *thy God,* **thou shalt find him**, *if thou seek him with all thy heart and with all thy soul.*

> **James 4:8a Draw nigh to God**, *and he will draw nigh to you.*

> **Colossians 1:10** *That ye might walk worthy of the Lord unto all pleasing, being fruitful in every good work,* **and increasing in the knowledge of God.**

II Peter 3:18a *But grow in grace, and* **in the knowledge of our Lord and Saviour Jesus Christ.**

Jeremiah 9:23–24 *Thus saith the* LORD, *Let not the wise man glory in his wisdom, neither let the mighty man glory in his might, let not the rich man glory in his riches: But let him that glorieth glory in this,* **that he understandeth and knoweth me,** *that I am the* LORD *which exercise lovingkindness, judgment, and righteousness, in the earth: for in these things I delight, saith the* LORD.

We don't know all the reasons that God wants us to know Him, but He says He does, and that is actually the only reason we need. If we just trust Him and discipline ourselves to study His Word so that we can find out as much as we can about our God and His Son, Jesus Christ, He will change us in many ways. Our part is to strive to know Him and to allow the Holy Spirit to use our knowledge of Him to affect our everyday lives.

BECAUSE GOD WANTS US TO LOVE HIM, AND WE CAN'T LOVE SOMEONE WE DON'T KNOW

God already loves us. Over and over in His Word, He gives us assurance of His great love for us in spite of our sinful condition.

I John 4:10, 19 *Herein is love, not that we loved God, but that he loved us, and sent his Son to be the propitiation for our sins. . . . We love him, because he first loved us.*

Ephesians 2:4–5 *But God, who is rich in mercy, for his great love wherewith he loved us, Even when we were dead in sins, hath quickened us together with Christ, (by grace ye are saved).*

Jeremiah 31:3 *The* LORD *hath appeared of old unto me, saying, Yea, I have loved thee with an everlasting love: therefore with lovingkindness have I drawn thee.*

John 3:16 *For God so loved the world, that he gave his only begotten Son, that whosoever believeth in him should not perish, but have everlasting life.*

He loves us so much that He was willing to give His life for us. Once we are saved, we become His children, and He then wants us to know Him so that we will love Him. In **Matthew 22:37** Jesus said, *"Thou shalt love the Lord thy God with all thy heart, and with all thy soul, and with all thy mind."* Is that possible to do when we don't even know Him? If someone you had never met were to tell you that she loved you, you would have a hard time believing her. Why? Because you don't know her, and she doesn't know you. In order for her to truly love you, she would have to get to know you and vice versa. As you develop a friendship and invest time, energy, and kindness, you may eventually grow to love each other.

Think about a special relationship in your life, maybe with your husband, sister, daughter, mother, or good friend. Any strong relationship requires that we spend time, communicate by talking and listening, share what we are going through in our daily lives, laugh together, think about each other, give sacrificially, express gratitude and praise, and enjoy being a part of each other's lives. That's how our relationship with God should be too. Of course, we must always be reverent in our dealings with Him, remembering that He is God and He is holy.

God wants you and me to have a close relationship with Him. **James 4:8** says, "*Draw nigh to God, and he will draw nigh to you.*" Just as we cultivate a relationship with someone we love, we should spend time with God in devotions and in church; speak to Him as soon as we wake up in the morning and in prayer throughout the day; read and obey His messages to us in His Word; ask Him for help and advice with problems; share fun thoughts with Him; praise and thank Him; give Him gifts of our tithes, offerings, and talents; and continually think of what would please Him.

Because God loves us, He wants us to grow in our love for Him as we develop our relationship with Him. The more we learn in God's Word about His character and all His kindness to us, the more our love for Him will grow. We are then to obey whatever He tells us in order to demonstrate our love for Him. **First John 2:3–5** says, "*And hereby we do know that we know him, if we keep his commandments. He that saith, I know him, and keepeth not his commandments, is a liar, and the truth is not in him. But whoso keepeth his word, in him verily is* **the love of God perfected**: *hereby know we that we are in him.*"

Because If We Don't Know the Truth About Our God We Will Believe Satan's Lies

We are in a war! Our enemy Satan wants us to lose. He is a very creative adversary in his attacks on us, and he doesn't play fair. One of

his favorite tactics is to lie to us about God. In **John 8:44** Jesus said of
Satan, *"He was a murderer from the beginning, and abode not in the truth,
because **there is no truth in him**. When he speaketh a lie, he speaketh of
his own: for **he is a liar**, and the father of it."*

Satan does not want us to know God because God is truth and His
words are truth. In some previous verses, **John 8:31–32**, Jesus said, *"If
ye continue in my word, then are ye my disciples indeed; and ye shall know
the truth, and the truth shall make you free."* God's truth gives us freedom
and victory over sin. On the other hand, Satan seeks to blind us with
his lies about God. Instead of the freedom and victory that can be ours,
he wants us to be defeated and in bondage. He delights in deceiving
us about the character of our God and wants us to believe that God
doesn't love us, that He is not good, not in control, not fair, not caring, and any other lie that he can convince us to believe. But **Daniel
11:32b** assures us that *"the people that do know their God shall be strong,
and do exploits."* In order to be victorious Christians who are able to
combat our enemy, we must know our Leader.

Because We Need to Be Sure That We Are Telling Others the Truth About God

In the Old Testament book of Job, Job's three friends sometimes un-
knowingly had a wrong or incomplete view of God. They believed
that God was punishing Job because of some unconfessed sin in his
life, and they spent three-fourths of the book trying to counsel Job
and convince him that they were right. The problem is that they were
not right. In **Job 42:7** God expressed His displeasure with Job's three
friends: *"My wrath is kindled against thee . . . for ye have not spoken of me
the thing that is right."* If we don't know our God, we could be guilty of
the same offense as Job's well-meaning friends.

Because God Has All the Answers to Life

Knowing God affects every aspect of our daily lives. **Acts 17:28** says,
"For in him we live, and move, and have our being." God has graciously
given us all the answers for life in His Word. When my husband, Ken,
and I were dating, there came a time that we discussed marriage. I remember the scene so well. We were at Bible Conference at our college,
and it was a gorgeous spring day. We were sitting on the grass under a

beautiful dogwood tree in full bloom. The sun was shining; the birds were singing; the spring flowers were impressing us with their color and lovely scents (very romantic!). But as we talked about marriage, I became fearful and said, "Ken, I'm afraid. I don't know anything about marriage, raising children, finances, or anything." He admitted that he was afraid too. He had not grown up in a strong Christian home, and I had come from a broken family. We both felt sadly ill-equipped to face the future. Then Ken said something very simple but extremely profound. He held up his Bible and said, "I'll tell you what. Let's just do whatever this Book says!" I answered, "That sounds good to me." We attempted (often feebly) to do that from then on. God kindly did not show us everything at once, and of course, we are still learning all the time. I will be the first to admit that we didn't always do things God's way, but it was the desire of our hearts. When Ken and I look back over many wonderful years of marriage, raising a family, and ministry, we believe that simple decision was probably the most important one we ever made as a couple.

Proverbs 2:1–5 tells us the wonderful benefits we will reap if we commit to study and search God's Word: "My son, *if thou wilt receive my words, and hide my commandments with thee; So that thou incline thine ear unto wisdom, and apply thine heart to understanding; Yea, if thou criest after knowledge, and liftest up thy voice for understanding; If thou seekest her as silver, and searchest for her as for hid treasures;* **Then shalt thou understand the fear of the Lord, and find the knowledge of God.**"

Ken often says that in the Bible are "the very words of God" to us. **Second Timothy 3:16** informs us that "*all scripture is given by inspiration of God, and is profitable for doctrine, for reproof, for correction, for instruction in righteousness.*" In His very own words, God gives us His book of instruction for living a righteous life. Among the many other wonderful things that it teaches us about God, the Bible is also God's "how to" book for life. Within its pages He teaches us how to love, how to communicate, how to deal with people, how to have a good marriage, how to manage finances, how to handle trials, how to bring up our children, how to work through a conflict, how to build friendships, how to control our tongues, how to encourage others, and a multitude of other life "how to's" because God has all the answers to life!

Second Peter 1:2–3 says, "*Grace and peace be multiplied unto you through* **the knowledge of God, and of Jesus our Lord**, *According as his divine power hath given unto us all things that pertain unto life and godliness,* **through the knowledge of him** *that hath called us to glory and virtue.*" Twice these verses tell us that God has given us everything we need to live a godly life "**through the knowledge of him.**" Knowing God truly does affect our everyday lives! A right view of God is necessary for us to please Him in each area of practical daily living. Since God has all of the answers to life, we must determine to simply obey Him with a willing heart.

BECAUSE "LIFE IS ALL ABOUT GOD. IT'S NOT ABOUT ME!"

I'm not sure where the above little saying originated, but I've heard several variations of it. We're all selfish and tend to think that life is all about "me and mine." It's not! **First Chronicles 29:11–13** emphasizes Who our God is and that life is all about Him. "*Thine, O LORD, is the greatness, and the power, and the glory, and the victory, and the majesty: for all that is in the heaven and in the earth is* **thine**; **thine** *is the kingdom, O* **LORD**, *and* **thou** *art exalted as head above all. Both riches and honour come of* **thee**, *and* **thou** *reignest over all; and in* **thine** *hand is power and might; and in* **thine** *hand it is to make great, and to give strength unto all. Now therefore, our* **God**, *we thank* **thee**, *and praise* **thy** *glorious name.*"

Isaiah 43:10b–11 says, "*That ye may know and believe me, and understand that I am he: before me there was no God formed, neither shall there be after me. I, even I, am the* LORD; *and beside me there is no Saviour.*"

God is God! He alone is to be exalted. As Christians, our purpose—the whole reason that God has created us—is to bring glory to Him with our lives. Often, it comes down to a decision: I have to decide if I'm going to bring glory to God by wholeheartedly obeying His Word or if I'm going to do what I want to do. A number of years ago, Ken came up with a little statement that has really been a help to our family:

Just two choices on the shelf,

Pleasing God, or pleasing self.

We have to make numerous daily choices about whether we want to live life God's way or please ourselves and do it our own way.

Since life is all about God and not about us, we should live all of life in the light of what we know about Him. Who He is should affect how we think and the way we live. We can't make right choices if we don't know Him.

What an amazing God! If we seek to know Him and live life His way, He so kindly promises that He will bless us. **Hebrews 11:6** tells us that "*he is a rewarder of them that diligently seek him.*" **Psalm 128:1–2** encourages us: "*Blessed is every one that feareth the LORD; that walketh in his ways. For thou shalt eat the labour of thine hands: happy shalt thou be, and it shall be well with thee.*" In **Psalm 119:2** we learn that "*blessed are they that keep his testimonies, and that seek him with the whole heart.*" And **II Peter 1:2** says that "*grace and peace*" will "*be multiplied*" to us "*through the knowledge of God, and of Jesus our Lord.*"

How Do I
Go About Knowing God?

A variety of devotional guides and books are written on the subject of knowing God. The notebook idea that I share with you is not the only way; it is just one simple tool that has been helpful to me as well as to others who have chosen to use it. Because of the impact that this study has had on me, whenever I have the opportunity to speak to other women, I generally share it with them. Almost weekly I have someone confide that this Bible study has made a difference in her life. One of the reasons that this study is so effective is that you are constantly searching God's Word to find out what it teaches about God, and that in turn helps you to concentrate on what you're reading. Do you ever find yourself mindlessly reading your Bible so that you can "check it off your list"? With this method of study, you will be diligently looking for truths about God that will help you know Him and grow in your relationship with Him.

I started by purchasing a notebook. I have found that a loose-leaf notebook is best because I can add pages as needed. I like using a 6½" X 9" notebook because it fits nicely with my Bible. I have friends who have done this on a computer, and if that works well for you, that's great. I tend to fear losing everything due to a computer crash. If you choose to use a computer, you will want to make sure you faithfully back up your files.

Then I began to read slowly through the book of **Psalms**, as my husband suggested, looking for anything that God told me about Himself. For example, in **Psalm 3:4** I discovered that God hears me: "*I cried unto the LORD with my voice, and he heard me out of his holy hill.*" To make this study more relevant to my life, I personalized each category; at the top of a new page in the notebook I wrote, **My God hears me**. I then wrote out all of **Psalm 3:4**. I continued through the book of **Psalms** looking for truths about my God. What a thrill to learn so many wonderful truths about Him: **My God is in control. My God is good. My God is great. My God is holy. My God loves me. My God is with me.** And so many others!

Each time I came across new information about God, I wrote it at the top of a new page and then wrote out the verse. As I continued in the study, I found numerous new categories as well as many verses that belonged under the categories I had already discovered. For instance, when I got to **Psalm 4:3**, I found another verse that needed to go under the category **My God hears me**: "*But know that the LORD hath set apart him that is godly for himself: the LORD will hear when I call unto him.*"

Often a verse will fit under more than one category. An example from **Psalm 100** is **verse 5**: "*For the LORD is good; his mercy is everlasting; and his truth endureth to all generations.*" I put this verse under the categories **My God is good, My God is merciful**, and **My God is Truth**.

If you keep the categories in alphabetical order, they are easier to find. (See Appendix A.)

Notebook dividers mark my "most used" categories. If you prefer, you can use the dividers for separating the categories alphabetically (example: A–C, D–F, etc.).

Underline the reference of each verse so that you can easily see where one verse ends and the next begins. This is also helpful when you are checking through a category to see if you already have a particular verse.

It's good not to be too much of a perfectionist as you work on the notebook. My notebook really isn't very pretty. There will be mistakes; the handwriting won't always be consistent; verses may be duplicated; there may even be some scratch-outs. However, if you spend too much

time recopying, reorganizing, and rearranging—trying to make it perfect—you'll lose sight of the goal for the project.

Be very careful not to use the verses out of context. This is the danger
of having the verses in categories, and we must always be sure that, as
one of my former pastors said, "The verse bears the weight of the whole
Scripture." Sometimes in the notebook I will put a little note in paren-
theses before or after the verse explaining who said it or explaining the
basic context of the passage. It's always a good idea to go back to study
the verse as it fits in the context of the passage before you share it or
use it to counsel someone. A reliable study Bible, commentary, or other
word study tool can be invaluable for gaining understanding of difficult
or unclear verses.

There are sample pages in Appendix B.

The categories I have in my notebook are not just attributes of God
the Father but are also qualities that we see in the example of God the
Son, Jesus Christ. **Colossians 2:9** says of Christ, "*For in him dwelleth
all the fulness of the Godhead bodily.*" God has told us to study Jesus and
to be like Him because God is *well-pleased* with His Son (**Mark 1:11**).
Romans 8:29 tells us "*to be conformed to the image of his Son.*" Some of
the categories I have chosen to add to my notebook are ones that encourage me toward that end:

> **My God wants me to love others.**
> **My God wants me to be obedient.**
> **My God wants me to be a servant like Jesus.**
> **My God wants me to praise Him.**

There are also categories that remind me about areas in my life that are
not pleasing to God:

> **My God hates pride.**
> **My God doesn't want me to judge others.**
> **My God hates** _____ (verses about things that God
> hates or is not pleased with).

And there are categories that instruct me:

> **What does my God say about my tongue?**
> **My God doesn't want me to be afraid.**

After I completed the book of **Psalms**, I went through **Proverbs**
and then through the whole Bible looking for more Scripture verses

about God and Jesus Christ. Once you are in the habit of looking for verses about your God, they will catch your attention when you are at church, at a Bible study, at retreats or conferences, reading a Christian book, and especially when you are having your personal devotions. When I don't have my notebook with me, I just jot the references down on a piece of paper and add the verses to my notebook later. I have been working on this study for over a dozen years and now have a notebook full of truth about my God. It is my most treasured possession.

If you are interested in starting your own notebook, I have given you a list (see Appendix A) of the categories I have in my notebook so far. I add new categories often because I'm always finding out more truths about my God. I've also given you a few of my favorite verses from each category to help you get started. Of course, it is best if you personalize and organize your notebook in a way that makes the most sense to you. For example, in my notebook I have combined some of the attributes of God that seem to overlap; I have **My God is great** and **My God is mighty** under the same category. Ken thinks that **My God is mighty** should go with **My God is strong**. Someone else might decide to make them three separate categories. It doesn't matter as long as your categories make sense to you and you can find the verses easily.

Having all of the verses on one aspect of God grouped together makes it easier for me to turn to whatever category I might need. If something unexpected comes into my life and I need assurance that God is in control, I can run to that section of my notebook. This has been helpful because it is not always possible to find the verses that you need in a concordance. For example, most of the verses in the category **My God is in control** don't even have the words *control* or *sovereign* in them (**Acts 17:24–25, 28**: "*God that made the world and all things therein, seeing that he is* LORD *of heaven and earth, dwelleth not in temples made with hands; Neither is worshipped with men's hands, as though he needed any thing, seeing he giveth to all life, and breath, and all things; . . . For in him we live, and move, and have our being*"). Whenever I need to be reminded that my God is in control, I can turn to over a hundred verses under that category (and that's just one example!).

WHAT DO I KNOW
About My God?

I eventually began to call my notebook **What Do I Know About My God?** The title came about because of an incident that a friend related to me about her two daughters. The girls were working at THE WILDS one summer and had just learned something very sad about a mutual friend. At first they just held each other and sobbed, but finally the older daughter grabbed her sister by the shoulders and said, "Okay, what do we know about our God?" They then worked through the problem in the light of what they knew about God.

When my friend shared that story with me, I was so impressed that these teen girls were able to run to what they knew about God to help them in their time of trial. I couldn't get the question that they had asked out of my mind: **"What do we know about our God?"** The question that normally comes to my mind when anything unexpected occurs in my life is "How does this affect me?" Sometimes I ask "Why?" or "Why me?" or "Why now?" Often I don't ask a question; I just panic or become fearful or frustrated. As I thought about it, I became convicted that my automatic tendency was to respond in the wrong way when something unexpected came into my life, and I realized that my thinking needed to change. That was when I decided to try to ask the question **"What do I know about my God?"** when anything unsettling occurs in my daily life. I had already been doing my notebook for a few years, so I had many verses at my disposal.

As we continue, I'll share some of the ways this has revolutionized my life.

WHAT DO I DO
With My Notebook?

REVIEW

Along with adding new verses and categories to the notebook, I regularly review the verses I have already written. I figure it doesn't do any good to have a notebook about God if I don't use it faithfully. Most days during my devotions or prayer time, I go back over the verses in one of the categories about God. Starting at the beginning of the notebook, I review the categories in order. If it is a longer one like **My God is great**, I might spend two or more days reviewing that subject. It has been helpful to use a paper clip or magnetic bookmark to mark where I left off. I continue through the entire notebook, rereading some of the verses each day and thinking about that attribute of God and how it should affect my thinking and my actions. When I get to the end of the notebook, I start over. If I'm going through a particular issue in my life and need to focus on a certain category, I take a side trip. Some days I spend my whole devotion time in my notebook and other days just a few minutes. The idea is to be constantly thinking about God and asking, **"What do I know about my God?"**

PRAISE

Whenever I hear anyone speak on prayer, he or she almost always gives the challenge to begin prayer time with praise. As I am reviewing an aspect of Who my God is, I find that my heart automatically begins to thank and praise Him for the way He demonstrates that attribute to me. If I'm reading the verses in the category **My God is compassionate**, I can praise Him for all of the many ways He shows me He cares specifically about my family and me. If I'm reviewing **My God is strong**, I can thank Him for the times He has given me the ability to go through difficult times or even through the sometimes tedious daily routine. Praying God's own words back to Him pleases Him, makes your prayer time more meaningful, and is another way to hide God's words in your heart.

The section **My God wants me to praise Him** is a very lengthy one. Because there are so many praise verses, I have labeled the pages "Monday, Tuesday, Wednesday, etc." I already have enough pages for two weeks of praising God. One day I underlined all the phrases in the verses that draw attention to something specific about God's character. It became obvious to me that God wants me to praise Him for Who He is and what He does instead of spending all my prayer time on requests. Now I try to begin my prayer time with a page of praise.

FOCUS

Quite often I find that I go to my notebook to get my focus back where it needs to be. Sharing an example of this might be the best way to explain. Ken and I were on our way to speak at a couples' retreat, and we really didn't feel as prepared as we'd like to have been. We were in the middle of moving to a different house, and things had been upside down in our lives for several weeks. I got out my notebook and read **My God is all-wise and gives me wisdom** out loud as we traveled. Here are some of the verses that we read:

> **James 1:5** *If any of you lack wisdom, let him ask of God, that giveth to all men liberally, and upbraideth not; and it shall be given him.*

> **Proverbs 2:6** *For the LORD giveth wisdom: out of his mouth cometh knowledge and understanding.*

> **Colossians 2:3** *In whom are hid all the treasures of wisdom and knowledge.*

We realized that it wasn't our efforts that make a retreat go well anyway (although it is our responsibility to prepare as well as we can); it's all up to God. He is the only One Who has wisdom and can help us. Knowing that God has the wisdom we needed comforted our hearts and put our focus back on Him instead of on our inadequacies. We were also encouraged to see God use His Word in the lives of the families at the retreat. **My God is all-wise.**

GRATITUDE

Seeing numerous verses grouped together all about one aspect of God causes me to reflect on that one particular aspect and, in turn, be full of gratitude. That's one of the reasons that I try to review a category each day.

One year around Christmas, I realized that I didn't have a category on **My God is a giving God**, so I excitedly started a new page. This has become one of my favorite sections, and each time I read through it, I am amazed at all of the verses that tell of God's gifts to His children. **James 1:17** tells us that *"every good **gift** and every perfect **gift** is from above, and cometh down from the Father of lights, with whom is no variableness, neither shadow of turning."* Here are just a few of the gifts that our giving God has given us.

God has **given** us *life and breath, and all things* (**Acts 17:25**).

He ***gave*** us *His only begotten Son* (**John 3:16**), and because of that gift, we can *have everlasting life.* (My category on salvation has well over one hundred verses.) How can we describe that most sacrificial of all gifts except in God's words: *His unspeakable gift* (**II Corinthians 9:15**)!

When Jesus left this world, He said that God would **give** us the Holy Spirit so that we wouldn't be alone: *"And he shall **give** you another Comforter, that he may abide with you forever; Even the Spirit of truth; whom the world cannot receive, because it seeth him not, neither knoweth him: but ye know him; for he dwelleth with you, and shall be in you"* (**John 14:16–17**). What an amazingly indescribable and comforting gift!

God also **gave** us His Word: *"All scripture is **given** by inspiration of God, and is profitable for doctrine, for reproof, for correction, for instruction in righteousness"* (**II Timothy 3:16**). What would we do without the gift of the Bible?

First Timothy 6:17 says that *"the living God . . . **giveth** us richly all things to enjoy"* (family, friends, food, health, rest, peace, rewards, nature, and countless other daily benefits). Wow!

There are many, many other things that God gives us and many verses that tell us that God wants us to be givers too. Just reading over all these "giving" verses at once makes me grateful and overwhelmed by God's goodness and His giving heart, and it challenges me also to be a giver. This is just one aspect of God that causes me to be grateful and appreciative for how good God is to His children.

ENCOURAGEMENT

Sometimes I use my notebook just to be encouraged or to think about God in relation to where I am or what I'm doing. While I was writing this section, Ken and I were hiding away at a cozy little oceanfront beach house that some kind friends had allowed us to use. It was January, so there were no bathing suits or umbrellas—only the seagulls and a few brave, bundled-up beachcombers or dog walkers. While at the ocean, I started a new section under **My God is the Creator** called **My God created the sea**. There are quite a few fascinating references about God's making and controlling the ocean. It was so special to go out on the beach for a walk and review all the verses about God and the sea.

Psalm 95:5 says, *"The sea is his, and he made it."* As I looked out on that beautiful, sparkling, immense body of water and pondered that fact, it struck me once again how awesome my God is and how finite I am. He **made** the ocean! When our electricity goes out at our house, we often lose our water too. Not only can I not make the sea, I can't even make enough water to fill my dishpan or my drinking glass!

Our mighty God controls all of creation, even the vast and incomprehensible sea. In **Matthew 8** Jesus calmed the storm and the disciples exclaimed, *"What manner of man is this, that even the winds and the sea obey him!"* Another verse in **Jeremiah 5:22** puts things into perspective: *"Fear ye not me? saith the* LORD: *will ye not tremble at my presence, which have placed the sand for the bound of the sea by a perpetual decree, that it cannot pass it: and though the waves thereof toss themselves, yet can they not prevail; though they roar, yet can they not pass over it?"*

In **Job 38:8–11** God tests Job with questions about creation: *"Or who shut up the sea with doors, when it brake forth, as if it had issued out of the womb? When I made the cloud the garment thereof, and thick darkness a swaddlingband for it, and brake up for it my decreed place, and set bars and doors, And said, Hitherto shalt thou come, but no further: and here shall thy proud waves be stayed?"* Ken has said that the sea is like a rebellious child that God put in a playpen so he can't get out (except with His permission). What a word picture! To know that such a great and powerful God is in control of every part of my little life and that He cares about me is truly comforting and encouraging.

LOVE

I have been taught that God's love for me will never change—He will always love me. I have also been taught that I should love the Lord with all my heart. I had a desire to do that, but if you're like me, I often wondered if I truly loved God with my whole heart and, if not, how I could change. Of course, we must keep our relationship with Him current, but another thing I have found is that the more I get to know my God, the more my love for Him grows.

First John 4:19 tells us that *"we love him, because he first loved us."* He really does love me and wants me to know and love Him. As I have been seeking to know Him, I am finding that it's hard not to love Someone Who

- Gave His only Son so that I could go to heaven. (**My God is my Savior.**)
- Forgives my sin even when I repeat the same dumb things over and over. (**My God forgives.**)
- Provides everything I need. (**My God provides.**)
- Is faithful to me even when I waver. (**My God is faithful.**)
- Knows me and cares about even the little things that I'm going through. (**My God is compassionate.**)
- Promises to always be with me. (**My God is with me.**)

I know that this will be an ongoing growth process, but in getting to know even a little about my God, I have seen my love for Him grow.

How Important Is My Thinking?

When I first started this study, I was actually having fun finding new verses on all of the facets that make up the character of God. It was a wonderfully eye-opening project, and I thoroughly enjoyed it. After a couple of years though, I saw that not only was it a special study but also it was changing me in ways that I hadn't even realized. Before I share more about my Bible study idea, I want to give a little of my testimony so that you might better understand my background.

I was not raised in a Christian home. My mom was a devoted stay-at-home mother, but she did not attend church. My dad was a non-practicing Catholic and a career army master sergeant. Because he was a gourmet cook, his job in the army was to manage the officers' or noncommissioned officers' club, which is like a country club. He was a kind, likeable, and generous man, but he was also a habitual drinker and a compulsive gambler. Dad was rarely at home, but when he was, he and Mom often had marital problems. Along with all of the normal military moving, we temporarily left my father a number of times throughout my growing-up years.

During this time, my mother was very interested in learning the truth about God. When I was in the fifth grade, she became involved with the cult of the Jehovah's Witnesses. (I even remember them coming to our house for regular studies.) However, God was at work in her life, and He had my father transferred to France, where she was removed from the influence of that group. On the army base there were only Protestant, Catholic, and Jewish services, so my mother sent my younger sister, Gail, my brother, Ron, and me to the Protestant Sunday school. One week they had a special promotional Sunday, and in order to get "points," we were encouraged to bring our parents to church. Being a dutiful mother (and after much begging on our part), Mom agreed to go with us. The chaplain preached a clear salvation message from God's Word, and God opened my mother's heart to the truth. **First Timothy 2:4–5** says, *"Who will have all men to be saved, and to come unto the knowledge of the truth. For there is one God, and one mediator between God and men, the man Christ Jesus."* That morning my beloved mother realized that she was a sinner, repented of her sin, and asked Jesus Christ to save her!

> **Romans 10:9–10, 13** *That if thou shalt confess with thy mouth the Lord Jesus, and shalt believe in thine heart that God hath raised him from the dead, thou shalt be saved. For with the heart man believeth unto righteousness; and with the mouth confession is made unto salvation. . . . For whosoever shall call upon the name of the Lord shall be saved.*

Her life was changed forever.

Dorothy Genovesi, my dear mother, was a good, loving, courageous mother and was a consistent example of a charactered life to us. She was always there for us—the "warm-cookies-waiting-for-us-when-we-came-home-from-school" kind of mom. In spite of difficult circumstances and her tumultuous marriage, she never became bitter, never let us know how hard her life had been, and never said unkind things about my dad. I'm sure we were affected by my father's absence, but we didn't seem to realize it because she loved us so much and always took such good care of us. She had a hunger to know the truth about God, and as soon as she was saved, she had a heart to grow and a desire for God's Word. God has been with her and given her strength and help all of these years. Even now in her eighties, she is a joyful, content, and growing Christian and an example to our family and others. I will ever be grateful to her and love her dearly.

When I was in the eighth grade, we returned to the States, and my baby Christian mother began to wonder if maybe we should be attending church somewhere. Graciously, God directed us to a Bible-teaching church (we saw a billboard near our home and decided to try it). It was there that Mom began to grow and serve. And it was there that I was saved at the age of thirteen during evangelistic services.

We left my father at the beginning of my senior year in high school due to some increased marital difficulties and moved to New Hampshire. When I graduated, I had no goals and no desire to go to college, and I didn't know what to do with my life. I was steeped in rock music, dating an unsaved guy, and knew very little about what the Bible taught. But God had plans for my life. The summer after I graduated, He sent a musical ministry team from Bob Jones University to our church. I was supposed to work that Wednesday night, but another employee "just happened" to ask me to trade nights with her, so I was able to go to prayer meeting. Mom and I watched the promotional film in amazement. We had no idea that there was such a thing as a Christian college. I was definitely impressed with all of the happy (especially male) faces.

After church, the young men on the ministry team insisted that I take a catalog and an application. I still had no intention of going to college, but we took the information home and my wise mother said, "Let's fill out the application just for fun." (I think she knew that I wasn't headed in a spiritually profitable direction.) When we got to the end of the form, we were instructed to send it in with a $20 registration fee, and I knew that the "fun" was over. My mom was trying to support our family of four on $80 a week after having been a stay-at-home mom most of her married life. But somehow, without my knowledge, she sacrificed the money and mailed the application.

That was in July, and in August, two weeks before school was to begin, I received an acceptance letter. I'm not sure how it all worked out, but before I knew it, my mother had let down the hems on my miniskirts (to comply with the dress standards of modesty), packed my bags, scraped up the money for a ticket, and put me on a plane headed to Bob Jones University in Greenville, South Carolina. I had never been south of the Mason-Dixon line and didn't know one soul at the school. When I finally realized what was happening, I panicked. But God was watching out for me. I saw a girl on the plane who was also wearing a long skirt and timidly asked her where she was going. She proudly replied, "Bob Jones University," and I quickly responded, "Help!" I discovered that Barb was a "mighty sophomore," and she confidently and kindly took me under her wing. When we arrived, she helped me get registered and situated. It didn't take any time at all for me to love it there because of all the friendly students and the wise and caring faculty.

Only God knows how I made it through four years of college and did so without a huge debt. But the greater wonder was that I began to learn how to live the Christian life. It was during those years that I learned that I should read my Bible and do what it said. It was there that I gained some direction for my life. And it was there that I met Ken and after graduation had the privilege of becoming his wife. As soon as we were married, we became full-time staff members at THE WILDS Christian Camp and have been serving there ever since.

I don't believe in using my background as an excuse for sin, but not being raised with the basics of the Christian faith as a child, I have seen that I have a lot of wrong ideas and thinking ingrained in my mind. Unless I am constantly meditating on God's Word and allowing it to change me, I will be guilty of wrong thinking and of being swayed by my feelings.

I have a dear friend Pat, whose husband underwent an unexpected open-heart surgery at the age of forty-six. I called her before the surgery to ask how I could pray, and she gave me the most amazing answer. I probably would have asked prayer for Ken to come through the surgery safely and successfully or that it wouldn't be as bad as they thought or for wisdom and strength for the doctors. Instead her response was "Mardi, pray that I'll think right." She just wanted to trust God and glorify Him no matter what course He chose for them to follow—even if He chose to take her husband home to heaven.

That really made an impression on me, and I realized how often we, as women, don't "think right." We tend either to believe Satan's lies about God or operate according to our feelings rather than believe the truth that God's Word tells us about our God. That's when we get into trouble. God wants us to "think Bible" instead of doing whatever we feel like doing or responding according to whatever mood we're in. He wants us to know Him so well that we can think about Him and then respond to a situation according to what we know about Him.

Dr. Amy Knicely has a little saying about controlling one's thoughts that has been helpful to me: "You do what you do, and you say what you say, because you think what you think." When I shared this statement with Ken, he added something that has further helped me: "You do what you do, and you say what you say, because you think what you think; and you think what you think because you believe what you believe about God, His Word, and yourself." It is vital that we know God and what He says in His Word so that we can think the way that He wants us to think and then please Him in what we do and in what we say.

One of the newer categories in my notebook is **My God wants me to "think right."** I was surprised at the number of verses on the mind, thinking, and thoughts, as well as the wonderful passages that help me to think right. It's obvious that God knows we struggle with wrong thinking. Many of these verses point us back to the importance of knowing our God.

> **Isaiah 26:3–4** *Thou wilt keep him in perfect peace,* **whose mind is stayed on thee***: because he trusteth in thee. Trust ye in the* Lord *for ever.*

> **II Corinthians 10:3–6** *For though we walk in the flesh, we do not war after the flesh: (For the weapons of our warfare are not carnal, but* **mighty through God** *to the pulling down of strong holds;) Casting down imaginations, and* **every high thing that exalteth itself against the knowledge of God***, and bringing into captivity every thought to the obedience of Christ.*

> **I Chronicles 28:9** (David's charge to Solomon) *And thou, Solomon my son,* **know thou the God of thy father***, and serve him with a perfect heart and with a* **willing mind***: for the* Lord *searcheth all hearts, and understandeth all the imaginations of the* **thoughts***.*

> **Philippians 2:5** *Let this* **mind** *be in you, which was also in Christ Jesus.*

I love **Philippians 4** when it comes to helping me practice right thinking.

> **Verse 4** *Rejoice in the Lord alway: and again I say, Rejoice.*

> **Verse 6** *Be careful [anxious] for nothing.*

Verse 7 *And the peace of God, which passeth all understanding, shall keep your hearts and minds through Christ Jesus.*

Verse 8 *Finally, brethren, whatsoever things are true, whatsoever things are honest, whatsoever things are just, whatsoever things are pure, whatsoever things are lovely, whatsoever things are of good report; if there be any virtue, and if there be any praise,* **think** *on these things.*

There are many other verses about our thinking, but it's clear that God wants us to keep our focus on Him so that He can clarify our fuzzy thinking.

Have you noticed that all of us have struggles, sinful tendencies, blind spots, areas of weakness, and strongholds (summed up in the word *sin*) in our lives that we have a hard time getting victory over? In his book *Changed into His Image*, Jim Berg says, "Our biggest problem . . . is not the environment in which we have been reared; it is not the evil that has been done to us by others; it is not the limitations that we feel so acutely. Our biggest problem is a heart that wants its **own way** in opposition to God's way."[1] **Isaiah 53:6** clearly points this out: "*All we like sheep have gone astray; we have turned every one to his own way.*"

For many years I was an "up-and-down person"—happy-happy one day and down in the dumps the next. It was also my tendency to over-react or fall apart in response to a circumstance or situation that wasn't according to my plan. My tongue can get me into trouble when I am critical, opinionated, negative, or judgmental. I could confess numerous other sins, but in short, when I do things "Mardi's way," I can be a real rascal.

I am finding that the more I learn about my God, the more I see the real me. As I focus on what God says about Himself in His Word, the Holy Spirit is slowly and kindly pointing out my sinful ways and wrong thinking and showing me that I need to change. It's not a pretty picture, but how much better it is to deal with it now instead of having to answer for it when I stand before God someday.

---

[1] Jim Berg, *Changed into His Image* (Greenville, SC: BJU Press, 1999), pp. 34–35.

I cannot study God without seeing myself in comparison to Him.

- As I see His greatness, I see my smallness. **(My God is great.)**
- As I see His control, I see my inability. **(My God is in control.)**
- As I see His strength, I see my weakness. **(My God is strong.)**
- As I see His holiness, I see my sinfulness. **(My God is holy.)**
- As I see His power, I see my helplessness. **(My God is powerful.)**
- As I see His righteousness, I see my disobedience. **(My God is righteous.)**
- As I see His humility and submission, I see my pride. **(My God wants me to be a servant like Jesus.)**
- As I see His giving heart, I see my stinginess or thoughtlessness. **(My God is giving.)**
- As I see His wisdom, I see my foolishness. **(My God is all-wise.)**

He is God! I am not. Ken once read a quote in a Sunday school class that made me smile and has a lot of truth in it: "There is a God in heaven, and you ain't Him." I am the one who must change to become more and more like Jesus. Jim Berg says that God "has made us dependent by design and must humble us. . . . There can be no biblical change without [humility]."[2] As I get to know God, He humbles me, and I see how fruitless and useless it is to try to live life in my own strength and how utterly dependent I must be on Him. Once again, what I am learning is "Life is all about God. It's not about me."

Even after more than twelve years of almost daily using my notebook full of Scripture to get to know God, I know that I have just barely seen the tip of the iceberg. Our God is so awesome that any study of Him is inexhaustible.

The founder of THE WILDS (and our mentor), Dr. Ken Hay, chose for our camp verse **I Corinthians 10:31**: *"Whether therefore ye eat, or drink, or whatsoever ye do, do all to the glory of God."* We can do that by knowing Him and His Word and allowing what we learn to change our wrong thinking and thereby our actions and life habits. This doesn't happen overnight because of the deeply rooted and habitual wrong thinking stemming from our backgrounds, our culture, our believing Satan's lies, the influences of others, and our own selfishness. That is

---

[2] P. 78.

why knowing God should be an ongoing lifelong study for all of us as we strive to grow in our relationship to Him and seek to bring glory to Him!

PART TWO

How Knowing God Is Changing My Thinking

How Knowing God
Is Changing My Thinking

I've explained how to start a notebook and how I use mine; now I want to share how knowing God is changing my life because of it. As I mentioned earlier, the first couple of years of using my notebook were a great thrill as I discovered many wonderful aspects of my God. Words cannot describe how overwhelming it is to start comprehending even a little of the goodness and greatness of God. But as I continued to add verses to my notebook, I began to notice that something else exciting was happening. At first I didn't realize it, but I began to see that what I was learning about my God was changing my thinking. I will spend the remainder of the book telling you what God has done in my life.

One of my concerns in sharing the things I have learned is that it will be too much about me. My heart's desire is to focus on **God** and how knowing **Him** is changing a sinner (me) and how it can help you too. Please understand that the purpose of this book is to encourage you to begin or to continue on a journey of knowing God, not to tell interesting stories. I am going to be transparent with you in my illustrations. I know that I'm a sinner, and I certainly don't want to glorify sin in any way. This has been such a life-changing process for me that I want to share with you how asking the question **"What do I know about my God?"** is helping me turn from my sinful habits and ways. These examples won't be earth-shattering, just nitty-gritty examples from everyday life. Please focus on the Bible verses and what they teach about God.

My God
Hates Pride

One of the first ways that I saw God changing my thinking was in the area of self-pity. Since I had not been taught biblical communication growing up, one of the main ways that I would handle my problems was by feeling sorry for myself. If things didn't go my way or if I thought I was right or had been wronged, I would pout. Ken is an absolutely wonderful husband, but sometimes I would get my feelings hurt, usually because of my expectations (which I would conveniently forget to tell Ken about) or if I thought I was right. Instead of communicating, I would give him the cold shoulder. We would go through the "What's wrong?"/"Nothing" routine on a regular basis. The poor guy never knew what would set me off.

I almost always pouted on Sunday nights after church. We have four children within a ten-year age span and live a thirty-minute drive from church. For a number of years Sunday was not my favorite day. It helped a lot when I made a decision to do as much preparation as possible on Saturday by having Sunday breakfast and dinner mostly ready and the clothes all ironed. But Sunday was still a hard, long day. We always had a nice, big Sunday dinner after church and then wouldn't eat supper until after Sunday evening church. Invariably, on Sunday night I would be in the kitchen trying to drum up something to eat while the rest of the family would be in the den laughing and having a good time. It was a perfect setup for a pout, and I would take advantage of it! The bottom line was that I wanted to punish my family because I had to work (after already working all day) while they were in the den having fun without me.

My "pouting" examples are numerous because it was one of "my ways" of handling life, but I think you can get the picture. I did it regularly and often. The interesting thing is that it never really solved any of my problems or disappointments, and it made life pretty miserable.

I have a sobering category in my notebook entitled **My God hates** _____ . Under that section, I put any verse that has to do with things that God hates or is displeased with. I had read the verses in **Proverbs 6:16–19** numerous times over the years, but one day the Holy Spirit used two of the verses to get my attention about pouting. **Verse 16** says, "*These six things doth the* LORD *hate: yea, seven are an abomination unto him.*" **Verse 17** begins the list, and the very first one is "*a proud look.*" I realized that pouting is "a proud look"! I put my nose in the air, don an air of superiority, and refuse to speak except when absolutely necessary and then in a cool tone of voice. When I am pouting, I want everyone to know that I have been hurt or offended or that I am right even if they won't acknowledge it. Pouting is pride. My focus is on me. I want my way, and someone is thwarting me.

The Lord used those verses to change me. The thought that my God hates pride has impacted me. I genuinely desire to please Him in my life. I don't want to practice something that He hates. Since He pointed out that verse to me in relation to pouting, I have seen a great deal of victory in this area. I still have a tendency to want to pout and don't always get an A+, but when I stop to think that my God hates pride, I ask Him to help me not to pout. And He does.

Another special thing that has happened is that I am enjoying my life so much more. I found that I had wasted a lot of time pouting and missed out on a lot of wonderful times with my family. God is also helping me to learn to communicate in a right way with my husband and children instead of sending backdoor messages. On Sunday nights I finally just asked if everyone could come out to the kitchen and be with me while I worked, and they were glad to. Ken also organized the family to pitch in so we could all go out to the den more quickly.

This principle about paying attention to the things that God hates can be helpful in other areas as well. Along with any kind of pride, He also hates lying, sowing discord among other believers (**Proverbs 6:17, 19**), complaining, imagining evil in our hearts against our neighbor (**Zechariah 8:17**), and various other sins. If we truly want to please God in our lives, we will take seriously anything that He says He hates and do everything we can to avoid those things.

My God Is My Father

We all crave meaningful relationships, and little girls seem to especially desire their daddy's love. I didn't grow up with a daddy who cared about me, and I was very insecure—always wanting approval and concerned about what people thought about me. I now know from studying the category **My God is my Father** that I wasn't insecure because I did not have a loving earthly father but because I did not know my loving heavenly Father. Even the godliest of fathers can't meet your deep, inner needs. Only God the Father can.

For those of us who don't have a father, **Psalm 68:5** tells us that He is *"a father of the fatherless,"* and **Psalm 10:14** says that He is *"a helper of the fatherless."* And of course, anyone who is born again is His child. What a comfort that **My God is my Father**! I can have a close relationship with Him. Once I am saved, He gives me all the benefits that a loving father gives his child.

He Has Taken Me into His Family

Ephesians 2:18–19 *For through him we both have access by one Spirit unto the Father. Now therefore ye are no more strangers and foreigners, but fellowcitizens with the saints, and of the household of God.*

Galatians 4:4–7 *But when the fulness of the time was come, God sent forth his Son, made of a woman, made under the law, To redeem them that were under the law, that we might receive the adoption of sons. And because ye are sons, God hath sent forth the Spirit of his Son into your hearts, crying, Abba, Father. Wherefore thou art no more a servant, but a son; and if a son, then an heir of God through Christ.*

He Loves Me

I John 3:1 *Behold, what manner of love the Father hath bestowed upon us, that we should be called the sons of God.*

He Chastens Me

Proverbs 3:11–12 *My son, despise not the chastening of the Lord; neither be weary of his correction: For whom the Lord loveth he correcteth; even as a father the son in whom he delighteth.*

He Takes Care of Me

Matthew 6:26, 32 *Behold the fowls of the air: for they sow not, neither do they reap, nor gather into barns; yet your heavenly Father feedeth them. Are ye not much better than they? . . . (For after all these things do the Gentiles seek:) for your heavenly Father knoweth that ye have need of all these things.*

He Protects Me and Keeps Me Safely in His Hand

John 10:29 *My Father, which gave them me, is greater than all; and no man is able to pluck them out of my Father's hand.*

I can trust Him because of Who He is, and therefore I have all of the security and love that I need. I used to think of God as Someone Who didn't have time for someone like me, Who couldn't possibly like me, and Who was waiting for me to trip up so that He could punish me. It is true that God is holy, just, righteous, and awesome and that we should fear Him, but as I've gotten to know Him more, I think of Him in a positive way—as my Father, as my Friend. **Psalm 56:9** states that "*this I know, for God is for me.*" I hope this doesn't sound too common or in any way irreverent, but whereas I used to be afraid of God, now, as I've gotten to know Him, I really like Him! He is my loving Father.

My God
Cares

This one is so sweet to me and goes along with **My God is my Father**. A good father takes care of his children, but he also cares about them. I have enjoyed having a heavenly Father Who cares about my daily life. I see it in so many different little ways, over and over. I'll just give you a couple of examples, and it's funny, but they both involve traveling and sleeping.

I was speaking at a ladies' retreat in Kansas and had tight plane connections, so it really wasn't a surprise when my luggage didn't arrive when I did. The retreat location was an hour and a half from the airport. I always keep my speaking notes and a little bit of make-up and my toothbrush in my carry-on bag and try to wear something that will be acceptable to speak in, but I didn't have any other clothes or toiletry items. My suitcase still hadn't arrived by bedtime, but several ladies helped me by providing some necessities. I was about to crawl into bed when I realized that I didn't have my pillow. I have some problems with my neck, so to avoid headaches, I always cram my own "squishy" pillow in my suitcase. Pillows in motels and at camps are generally of the harder foam variety, and the one on my bed was no exception. I happened to look up and saw another pillow on top of a shelf in the room. When I checked it, it was a "squishy" pillow! I thanked God for taking care of me and for caring about little things. (My luggage showed up in time for the morning session, and I woke up without a headache.)

The second example did not involve me, but it involved my family, so it affected and comforted me to see God's care so clearly and evidently illustrated. Our oldest son, Matt, and his wife, Kelly, are involved in a unique ministry called Camps Abroad. They go to foreign mission fields and spend a few weeks helping missionaries in their camping endeavors by teaching biblical philosophy of camping, training the camp leaders and counselors in effective counseling techniques, and helping them run an exciting program. It is a thrilling and rewarding ministry, but they must deal with international travel, new people, unfamiliar food, varying cultures, language barriers, climate and time adjustments, pesky critters, lack of hygiene and the resulting threat of disease, and numerous other unusual and challenging situations.

On one trip Kelly had to travel back from Africa by herself when she was seven months pregnant with their first child. We were all concerned because she would be traveling alone, would have two eight-hour flights plus layovers, and would get very little sleep. Several of us were praying that God would take special care of her. She had requested an aisle seat so that she could get up to walk without disturbing anyone, but somehow the airline had not fulfilled the request. Matt tried to get it straightened out, and she eventually did get an aisle seat on the first leg of the journey. However, when Kelly was ready to board for the second part of the trip, she discovered that they had switched her seat again. After she very sweetly explained her situation, they asked her to have a seat in the waiting area. Finally, a man handed her a new seat assignment, and she boarded the plane. Imagine her surprise when she ended up in the business class section of the airplane. We know it as first-class! She had a reclining seat, the current London morning paper, upgraded menus with deliciously prepared food served on real china, fresh fruits, juices, chocolates, any-time snacks, warm wet washcloths, and attentive flight attendants. Her favorite touch was fresh roses in the restroom! She was gratefully able to get up and stretch, sleep, eat well, and most of all rejoice in God's goodness. We were thrilled when we learned of God's kind care of our Kelly and chuckled over all the "extras" that He had bestowed.

Matthew 10:29–31 *Are not two sparrows sold for a farthing? and one of them shall not fall on the ground without your Father. But the* very hairs of your head are all numbered. Fear ye not therefore, ye are of more value than many sparrows.

I Peter 5:7 Casting all your care upon Him; for he careth for you.

My God
Is the Creator

We live in the peaceful mountains of North Carolina, and I like to go for daily walks and enjoy the creativity of God. Often I will see some charming bit of nature that God has created and be reminded of what an amazing God we have. One fall my attention was drawn to all the different colors, shapes, and varieties of mushrooms that He has made. When I went on my walks, I saw pink, curly mushrooms; a red mushroom with polka dots; mushrooms that look like little paper umbrellas; a leatherlike mushroom; a mushroom that looked just like a banana; fluffy fan-shaped mushrooms; smooth, brilliant yellow mushrooms; and perfectly round, barbell-like white mushrooms with raised white dots. They grow so quickly that they seemed to crop up before my very eyes. We even had one mushroom in our driveway that managed to push up through the asphalt. Only God could give that little fungus the ability to do that!

God's creative genius is inspiring. On my walks I can observe changing trees and obscure little flowers, unique bugs and scary spiders, splendid butterflies with intricately designed wings, gorgeous or interesting skies, and all manner of fascinating creatures. All of them point me to my great and unlimited Creator. The psalmist was also inspired by God's handiwork. **Psalm 104:24** says, "O LORD, how manifold are thy works! in wisdom hast thou made them all: the earth is full of thy riches."

Even birds have become a joy to me. I had never been a big bird person until I had to speak at a mother/daughter banquet on the theme of birds. As I studied them, I gained a new appreciation of God's boundless imagination. Since then, I have enjoyed listening to God's creativity in the endless variety of songs His little birds sing. Most of the birds' songs are cheerful and enthusiastic, and they remind me to be excited about praising God too. **Psalm 150:6** could be the bird's verse or mine: "*Let every thing that hath breath praise the LORD. Praise ye the LORD.*"

But God's creativity does not just apply to nature; it also applies to people. We tend to think that we should all fit into a similar mold, and when we don't, we can find ourselves questioning Him. I have always been a very average person—in appearance, in abilities, in intelligence—but have managed to be around people who are exceptional. I have never felt as if I was good at anything in particular. When I was younger, I had a problem with my complexion and my figure and would always envy pretty girls. Even as I got older, I struggled because I didn't think I measured up. I was never as capable, as popular, as smart, as talented, as attractive, or as organized as many of my friends.

It is such an easy thing to compare ourselves to others, isn't it? As women, we manage to compare all kinds of things—personality, weight, height, hair, fingernails, complexion, talents, abilities, cars, homes, clothes, children, husbands, and even spirituality. You name it; we compare it.

The verses in the category **My God is the Creator** have helped me in this struggle. **John 1:3** tells us that "*all things were made by him; and without him was not any thing made that was made.*" **Psalm 139:14–16** gives me a right perspective: "*I will praise thee; for I am fearfully and wonderfully made: marvellous are thy works; and that my soul knoweth right well. My substance was not hid from thee, when I was made in secret, and curiously wrought in the lowest parts of the earth. Thine eyes did see my substance, yet being unperfect; and in thy book all my members were written, which in continuance were fashioned, when as yet there was none of them.*"

Psalm 100 is my favorite psalm. **Verse 3** says, "*Know ye that the LORD, he is God: it is he that hath made us, and not we ourselves.*" Knowing that God is God, that He is my Creator, and that He made me (and my children too) exactly the way He wanted to make me (and them) has been a great comfort to me. It has helped me to be more content with the way God made me because if He made me this way, He will use me the way I am. I need to work with what God has given me, change the things that can be improved, and then get my focus off myself and onto God and others. Instead of wanting to be like someone else, I can focus on what **Psalm 100:2** tells me to do, and that is to *"serve the Lord with gladness"* in whatever way He allows me to serve.

MY GOD
Is in Control

I have Italian blood (an excuse) and am a bit of a hyper person. I tend to react negatively if my schedule gets interrupted or doesn't go the way I had it planned. (It's called sin.) In studying Jim Berg's book *Changed into His Image*, I have been taught that this is another one of the ways that I want my "own way." I generally wake up in the morning and have my list of things to accomplish or at least a mental idea of how my day should go. Now you and I both know that life generally does not work that way. The result: frustration and distress.

A number of years ago, Jim's wife, Pat, spoke to our staff ladies and shared an illustration that has really helped me with this problem. She talked about how we expect our lives to be similar to going through a cafeteria line, where we can choose exactly what we want to eat. When I go through a cafeteria line, I might pick strawberries, broccoli with cheese sauce, trout amandine, and a bran muffin. I would definitely pass on the liver and turnip greens. In our lives we like to choose the way our life or our day will turn out. We have a basic plan in mind of how our lives should work: "I will grow up in a happy home. I will go to college and meet the man I'm going to marry by the time I'm a junior. We'll get married as soon as we graduate. After two years we will have a baby boy, and after two more years we will have a baby girl; no more children. We'll pass on the financial problems, and definitely NO health problems." Our little plan sounds great, but realistically it just isn't the way life works. Instead, as Pat said, God intends for our lives to be more of a blue-plate special, like the old school lunch lines where our food was just handed to us. God has a special plate prepared for me each day, and that plate might have liver or turnip greens on it. Even though it might not be my favorite thing, God knows what I need and what's best for me, not only for my life but for each day as well.

This idea has really helped me. As I studied **My God is in control,** I came across many impacting verses, but two especially changed my thinking. **Psalm 18:30** says, "As for God, **his way** is perfect: the Word of the LORD is tried: he is a buckler to all those that trust in him." And then **verse 32:** "It is God that girdeth me with strength, and maketh **my way** perfect." My God knows what's best for me. I can trust Him with every part of my life, the little things as well as the big ones. And He will give me strength to deal with whatever He puts on my plate.

This particular category especially affects my thinking because there are so many things that come into my day, as well as my life, that don't turn out exactly the way I expect them to. Life certainly is not dull or boring! It offers many twists and turns, from the unexpected bout with the flu, to the traffic delay, to having to search for those lost keys, to the church conflict, to your husband's needing you to do an important errand that wasn't on the list, to the heart-stopping phone call, to the stubborn toddler who needs consistent discipline, to the washing machine breaking on the day that you have six loads of laundry to do, to the friend who needs a listening ear, to the diagnosis that you don't want to hear, to the teenage daughter who's had her feelings hurt, and on and on it goes.

One of the wonderful results of realizing that my God is in control of my day and my life and relinquishing them to Him has been that I am not nearly as hyper and distressed when my schedule is changed, and I find myself enjoying my life so much more. I could give you many examples from my daily life, but I'll share just three.

We have just finished the stage in life when our children were involved in a variety of activities. One of our children was involved in a competition, and things did not turn out the way we had hoped. I won't give you details, but many of you have been in those types of situations. You and your child invest a lot of time, money, and energy, and then because of circumstances and the human factor, your hopes are dashed and your child is disappointed. In our particular situation, the results didn't seem fair, and a number of other people agreed with us. Then came the battle. I went through all the agonizing thoughts: "I can't believe this!" "It seems so unfair." "I wish that . . ." "If only they hadn't . . ." "I wonder if we could . . ."

That night as my friend and I drove home from the competition (her child was involved too), we were hashing through the events of the day and desperately trying to help each other think in a way that would please God. It wasn't easy. When I have sinned, I can deal with the consequences because I know that I deserve them. But when things seem unjust, especially when it involves my children, I have a harder time (the ol' Mama Bear syndrome). My friend immediately quoted **Psalm 115:3**: *"But our God is in the heavens: he hath done whatsoever he hath pleased."* We referred to that verse over and over in the next days for our children and ourselves. When I got home, I got out my notebook and went right to the section **My God is in control**. The verses calmed my spirit, turned my thinking in the right direction, and made me focus on my sovereign God instead of the circumstance that I could not control. No matter what I thought about the situation that we found ourselves in, God had allowed it. Life is not always fair. It certainly wasn't for Joseph (**Genesis 37–50**) or for our greatest example, Jesus, but God always uses our circumstances for good.

As I reflect back on that time, I see that the many life lessons that we learned from this event have far exceeded what might have been gained by winning a competition. God loves us and knows what we need, and He controls even the minor aspects of our lives. **Isaiah 46:9–11** says, *"Remember the former things of old: for I am God, and there is none else; I am God, and there is none like me, Declaring the end from the beginning, and from ancient times the things that are not yet done, saying, my counsel shall stand, and I will do all my pleasure: . . . yea, I have spoken it, I will also bring it to pass; I have purposed it, I will also do it."*

Not too long ago I had a car accident. It was my fault. I was about an hour and a half away from home at a busy intersection during rush hour traffic, trying to turn in to a shopping center parking lot. Eventually I thought it was clear to go, but it wasn't. Someone crunched into my back fender; the car spun and slammed into the curb. No one was hurt, but our car was totaled. My first reaction was to fuss at myself for being so dumb. My second was to ask, **"What do I know about my God?"** I'm not sure why, but **Ecclesiastes 7:13** immediately came to my mind: "*Consider the work of God: for who can make that straight, which he hath made crooked?*" It made me laugh, but it also put things into perspective for me about who was in control. I was then able to give tracts to the policeman and the person who hit me and not question why God had allowed the accident.

This third story is a little lengthy, but it is one of my favorite life memories. It illustrates how knowing that my God is in control, even in the minor events of life, can help and change us.

We were entering one of the busiest weeks of our married life. Have you ever noticed how events can come in bunches? Our oldest son, Matt, was getting married at the end of the week on Saturday, January 31.

Our third son, Aaron, was graduating from high school in May, but because he went to a public school, we were having our own senior trip with the other seniors from THE WILDS. This trip had been on the calendar before the wedding and was scheduled for Sunday, January 25, through Tuesday. We had toyed with not going because of all that had to be done for the wedding on the following Saturday but decided that Aaron's senior trip was extremely important too, and even though the timing was not the best, we would do whatever was necessary to make both events special. One other event occurred that week too—January 27 was our twenty-fifth wedding anniversary.

I had a huge list of things to get done before the wedding but decided that I would try to set it aside and really enjoy the senior trip. Our entourage included eight juniors and seniors in a van driven by one of our younger staff men, Steve Stodola (plus his wife and nine-month-old baby), and seven sets of parents in five different cars. Ken and I drove our own car because we were planning to do some wedding errands on the way home. Our destination was only three hours away in Gatlinburg/Pigeon Forge, Tennessee.

One of the fathers, Rand Hummel, had done a great job planning and arranging the trip, and we had a ball! There were a lot of fun activities such as go-carts, miniature golf, and laser tag in the dark with all of us running around "lasering" each other. Rand had put together a video,

"Scrapbook of Memories," on each of the teens. The fathers took turns presenting challenging devotionals, and testimony times when the teens and parents shared their hearts were touching. Most of the students had been together since they were babies, so you can imagine the nostalgia involved: lots of memories, lots of laughter, lots of tears!

The plan for Tuesday was to have one last time of testimonies and devotions and then to do our two final fun events and head home in the early afternoon. After waking up that morning, I was in the motel bathroom when I heard Ken calling for me to come quickly. I thought that maybe there was some big news story he wanted me to see, but when I hurried out, what I saw shocked me. Ken had thrown open the curtains, and it was snowing the biggest flakes that I had ever seen. They seemed at least three inches in diameter and were coming down hard!

My first thought was the wedding. I started to panic and said to Ken, "Hon, the wedding! What are we going to do? We can't get stuck here. Quick! Throw everything in the suitcase and let's get out of here right now. " Ken is always wonderfully calm, and he kindly told me to settle down, that we would listen to the weather report, and then the men would decide what to do.

Then it clicked. I thought, "Okay, Mardi, he's right. **What do you know about your God?**" For some reason I didn't have my notebook with me, and in my panicked state, I couldn't think of what to look up in my Bible. I decided to look up the word *snow*. I came across two verses that really helped me. **Psalm 148:8** says, "*Fire, and hail; snow, and vapour; stormy wind fulfilling his word.*" **Job 37:6** says, "*For he saith to the snow, Be thou on the earth.*" Just those simple verses made me realize that God made the snow. God is in charge of the weather. Those monster snowflakes were not a surprise to Him.

Then, in spite of what was coming, I was able to give my schedule to God and accept whatever He chose to put on my plate that day (and the days ahead). I decided that I would relax, enjoy the day, and trust God; He would take care of the wedding. **My God is in control!**

That is not the end of the story. The weather report said that the snow would turn to rain in the afternoon, so the men decided to eliminate one activity but to otherwise proceed with the schedule. The devotional and testimony time with the seniors was again touching and memorable. Next came the activity and a bit of nervousness as the snow continued coming down quickly and furiously. Around noon the men decided that maybe we had better hit the road. They had a powwow with the teens and suggested that we all have lunch, but the teens wanted to wait to eat in Asheville, which was about an hour and a half away. When we stopped for gas, everyone went into the little convenience store and bought a few snacks. Then off we went on our momentous mountainous journey on the notorious I-40—with the snow still falling.

I am sure you know what is coming. We were "Snowbound on I-40!" (I still have a copy of the newspaper with this prominent front-page headline.) We were stuck in a twelve-mile traffic jam for twenty-four hours. The snow continued all night, accumulating to a total of sixteen inches. We raided our suitcases, layered all the clothes and socks we could find, and turned the car on for ten minutes every hour to take the chill off. One of the couples took Baby Kristy and her mother in with them and ran the car a good part of the night. They never ran out of gas, and little Kristy slept nine hours straight.

What a memory! I don't know anyone else who has spent their twenty-fifth anniversary night stranded in a car on I-40. We ate Triscuits and Farley's Fruit Snacks for our anniversary meal. (We debated whether to eat our one bag of M&M's but decided to save it for posterity.) But do you know that it turned out to be a very special time for us as a couple? We certainly weren't going anywhere, so we used the time to rehearse God's goodness to us over the years and took turns praying for everything and everyone that came to mind. What a thrill it was to look back on what God had done in twenty-five years and to thank Him! God allowed us to stop in the midst of our busyness and fun to consider Him. In **Psalm 46:10** He reminds us to "*be still, and know that I am God: . . . I will be exalted in the earth,*" and we had the privilege to do just that.

Since no one had eaten lunch and would miss supper and possibly other meals, all of the parents sent as much food as possible to the van with the teens. At 4:30 a.m., one of the parents, Dave Cleary, decided to do some scouting and located a truck stop about a mile down the road. He went back to the van at 5:00, roused all of the teens, and hiked them up to the café for a hot breakfast. Since the restaurant was low on help, and since all of our teens had worked in the camp kitchen and dining hall, they volunteered to waitress, wash dishes, and man the kitchen. THE WILDS food service manager, Cal Mair, was also on the trip, so he donned a truck stop shirt and hat and became a short-order cook. Ken was concerned about the elderly people stranded in their cars, so he bought a bunch of honey buns to distribute. We had only Christmas tracts with us but gave one with each honey bun and wished each person a "Merry *after* Christmas." Everyone worked hard until the traffic finally started moving again around 1:30 p.m. on Wednesday. What a special way for our kids to end their senior trip—helping others!

This experience ended up being one of my favorite memories ever. Knowing that my God is in control and that He put snow and a twenty-four-hour delay on my plate made a difference. If I had decided to pout, complain, and fret, I would have missed out on a wonderful experience and a treasured memory with my husband and son. And do you know what else happened? When we returned home, our friends pitched in to help us. My wedding "to do" list got done, and Matt and Kelly were happily married three days later.

I know these illustrations may seem silly, but the simple fact that my God is in control over every aspect of my daily life, large or small, has truly made a tremendous difference. If we could get into the habit of realizing that every little interruption, every circumstance, every person, every trial, everything that comes into our lives has been sent by God, then when the major life events occur, we would be ready to rest in the fact that He is in control. If we truly believe that and trust Him, we will have peace, calmness, and joy in the midst of whatever God sends. **What do I know about my God?**

> **Psalm 135:5–6** *For I know that the* LORD *is great, and that our Lord is above all gods. Whatsoever the* LORD *pleased, that did he in heaven, and in earth, in the seas, and all deep places.*

My God is in control!

My God Is Trustworthy
And Wants Me to Trust Him

Do you have a difficult time trusting God? If we're honest, many of us will have to respond with a sheepish yes. My big struggle for many years was in the area of finances. As young families say, "More month at the end of the money" was true more often than not. However, over the years I have found that God always provides and I should not worry about it.

> **Philippians 4:19** *But my God shall supply all your need according to his riches in glory by Christ Jesus.*

For the most part I have learned to trust God with the finances, but unbelief has a habit of resurfacing from time to time.

One of the things God has asked those of us who are married to do is to submit to our husbands. **Ephesians 5:22** says, *"Wives, submit yourselves unto your own husbands, as unto the Lord."* **First Peter 3:5** says, *"For after this manner in the old time the holy women also, who trusted in God, adorned themselves, being in subjection unto their own husbands."* Submission is not a hard thing when you agree with your husband; of course, then it isn't actually submission. Submission comes into play when we disagree. Ken and I get along wonderfully and usually agree. (By the way, when a husband and wife have both determined to do what the Bible says, they find themselves "on the same page" the majority of the time.)

A couple of years ago in the early fall we had decided that our car was getting up in mileage and that we should start looking for a different one the first of the year when it would be more financially feasible. The problem came when a friend found the perfect car for us four months earlier than we had planned. It was an amazing deal, had very low mileage, was in excellent condition, had a tape player and power locks (which we desired), and was even a beautiful color. We both fell in love with it. After some prayerful consideration, Ken decided that we should pursue the purchase. He wanted a more dependable car for my frequent trips up and down the mountain roads and knew that we had several longer trips coming. He also thought that the Lord had provided just the right car for our needs. I was hesitant and thought that maybe we should wait because of the finances. We had a medical bill that was $1000 more than we had thought it would be, and that had taken away from the car fund. So, we didn't agree, and I started to worry that my husband was making a wrong decision.

It was time for me to submit. I went back to my verses on submission, spent time in my notebook going over the applicable verses, and decided that I needed to submit *"as unto the Lord."* Even if I didn't agree with the decision, I needed to trust that God would take care of the situation. My job was to submit to my husband with a sweet attitude and not to bring it up for any further discussion.

Well, we got the car, and Ken drove me to Florida to speak at a ladies' retreat. Unbeknown to me, before the retreat even began (probably while I was struggling with submitting), the women had taken a special love offering for the speaker. It was a huge gift, and I was totally overwhelmed by their generosity and God's provision. It helped take care of the bills and, of course, strengthened my faith. Then, a couple of months later a dear friend gave us a gift that took care of the rest of the car payment! How humbled I was by God's goodness. How grateful I was that I had submitted to my husband and trusted my God! But even if it hadn't worked out that way, I should still trust my God. **Psalm 34:8** says, *"O taste and see that the LORD is good: blessed is the man that trusteth in him."*

Maybe you have a hard time trusting God because of some trial that He has allowed in your life. Possibly something has turned your life upside down, or something has occurred that doesn't seem fair, or something has happened that you just don't like. Life is full of trials. Ken says that people are either in the middle of a trial, coming out of a trial, or getting ready to go into a trial. Really, there are only two choices for us as Christians: either we trust God or we don't. We can go through the trial depending on God, or we can chafe under it and complain and be miserable. We have to choose.

In the book of Job, we find the story of a man who went through unfathomable trials when he lost all ten of his children, many servants, all of his livelihood and wealth, and his health. Job was a man of integrity, who had been blessed by God and did not understand what had suddenly happened. (It was, in fact, a test of his faith, but it's quite possible that Job never knew that while on earth.) Job's famous words in **Job 13:15** are a rebuke to us when we stagger: *"Though he slay me, yet will I trust in him."* Job did trust God, but he also went through times of doubt. And do you know what God did? In the closing chapters of Job, God deftly drew Job's attention back to Who God is and what He does until Job humbly acknowledged in **Job 42:2, 6**: *"I know that thou canst do everything. . . . Wherefore I abhor myself, and repent in dust and ashes."*

When Ken was teaching the book of Job, he made a statement that has been a big help to me: "When there's a gap between God's way and wisdom and my understanding of God's way, I must fill the gap with trust."

> **Psalm 28:7** *The LORD is my strength and my shield; my heart trusted in him, and I am helped: therefore my heart greatly rejoiceth.*

I can trust my God!

My God
Guides and Leads

Along with learning about trusting God, our family has been experiencing the fact that God leads and guides His children. Looking back over your life and rehearsing what God has done can cause great gratitude, but it's also exciting to watch it unfold in the present. For the last several years our three sons, and our daughter as well, have been going through the stage of life when they are making major life-altering decisions. They have been getting their education, choosing spouses, and trying to determine what God wants them to do and where He wants them to serve. While they were small children, we began praying about their marriage partners, and it's been so much fun to see God provide the girls that perfectly compliment each of our sons. We asked the boys to look for girls who loved God and were teachable, and God brought them true gems who have greatly enriched their lives (and ours!).

It has also been fascinating to see how God has led them as they study His Word, pray, and sort through what they should do with their lives, where He wants them to go, and the timing of it all. There are wonderful verses that assure us that God has a unique plan for each of us, and if we acknowledge Him, commit our way to Him, and trust in Him, He will order our steps and direct our paths. I've certainly seen it to be true in my life.

Proverbs 3:5–6 *Trust in the* LORD *with all thine heart; and lean not unto thine own understanding. In all thy ways acknowledge him, and he shall* **direct thy paths.**

Psalm 37:5, 23 *Commit thy way unto the* LORD*; trust also in him; and he shall bring it to pass. . . . . The* **steps of a good man are ordered** *by the* LORD*: and he delighteth in his way.*

Psalm 23:3a *. . . he* **leadeth** *me in the paths of righteousness for his name's sake.*

Our second son, Evan, and his wife, Natalie, after much prayer and preparation, believe that God wants them to start a church in the Boston area. Time after time as we have watched and prayed, we have seen specific answers to our prayers for guidance. We have seen Him answer prayer about the timing of the move to Massachusetts, about the adjustment of the family to a new culture, for affordable housing, for provision of financial support and a job with health insurance, in the narrowing down of a possible location, by providing core people who desire to help start a new ministry, by sending people to reach out to and working in their hearts. Evan and Natalie have more questions about the future, but it's been comforting to know that God is there, that He has a plan, and that He is at work giving direction one step at a time. It's been exciting to see what God is doing in their lives as well as in the lives of the rest of the family. He is at work!

There is much encouragement and security in the promise of **Psalm 48:14**: *"For this God is our God for ever and ever: he will be our* **guide** *even unto death."*

MY GOD
Is My Shepherd

Because I am a sinner, I sin. Do you ever get discouraged when you see an area of growth in your life but then find yourself failing once again? I get upset with myself when I do that and think that God must be tired of me, even disgusted sometimes. A study of the Shepherd and the sheep has been such an encouragement to me.

Jesus is the Good Shepherd. **John 10:11, 14** say, "*I am the good shepherd: the good shepherd giveth his life for the sheep. . . . I am the good shepherd, and know my sheep, and am known of mine.*" We are the little sheep. **Psalm 100:3** tells us that "*we are his people, and the sheep of his pasture.*" Sheep are rascally and fearful and wayward and dumb. **Isaiah 53:6** gives us a good picture of sheep: "*All we like sheep have gone astray; we have turned every one to his own way.*" In spite of that, Jesus loved His little sheep so much that He was willing to die for them. No matter how much trouble the sheep cause, the Shepherd loves them, sacrifices for them, and does whatever is necessary to care for and provide for them. **Psalm 23:1** says, "*The LORD is my shepherd; I shall not want.*"

One of my favorite illustrations is that of the "cast" sheep, from Phillip Keller's book *A Shepherd Looks at Psalm 23* (a wonderfully helpful book for studying the Good Shepherd and the sheep). The foolish little sheep wanders off and will eventually lie down in the lush green grass, roll over on her side, and become unbalanced. This causes her to flip

upside down with her legs flailing frantically in the air. She has become
"cast." This situation is extremely dangerous because of predators and
exposure, but it is also life-threatening because gases build up in her
system and expand so that circulation is eventually cut off. Death can
come within a few hours on a hot day. The sheep is completely helpless
and can be saved and restored only by the loving care of the shepherd.
When the shepherd finally finds her, he doesn't just quickly jerk the
sheep back onto her feet, yell at her, and send her on her way. He
must carefully turn her over, then gently massage her legs, and slowly
help her get back on her feet. Throughout the restoration process, the
shepherd is lovingly and tenderly talking to the wayward one. If she is
in bad shape, he may even have to carry her back to the fold, which
is the picture we so often see of the shepherd with the little sheep on
his shoulders. This is a beautiful and touching representation of how
our loving Good Shepherd wants to deal with us when we stray or fail.
Psalm 23:3 says, "*He restoreth my soul.*" What a vivid word picture of
our Savior's love for us.

I have had a lifelong struggle in certain areas and tend to think God
must get fed up with me. There has been steady growth over the years,
but I still have a long way to go and have to go back to God over
and over to confess my sin and ask forgiveness. I am so grateful for
my Good Shepherd, who loves me and willingly and kindly "*restoreth
my soul*" even when I fail so often. I picture myself as that fluffy little
sheep that will do just fine as long as she stays right behind the Good
Shepherd but can be in big trouble if she wanders away and ends up
cast.

One of my categories is **My God forgives**, and there are many verses
that assure me of God's willingness to forgive me when I repent and
confess my sin.

> **1 John 1:9** *If we confess our sins, he is faithful and just to forgive us
> our sins, and to cleanse us from all unrighteousness.*
>
> **Psalm 86:5** *For thou, LORD, art good, and ready to forgive; and
> plenteous in mercy unto all them that call upon thee.*
>
> **Psalm 103:3, 12** *Who forgiveth all thine iniquities; who healeth all
> thy diseases. . . . As far as the east is from the west, so far hath he
> removed our transgressions from us.*

Not too long ago I was sharing these thoughts about little sheep and the Shepherd at a ladies' retreat and a couple of the ladies gave me some adorable little stuffed sheep. I have one of them where I can see it each day when I have my devotions, another one in our bedroom, another in the living room, and one upside down (cast) on my kitchen windowsill. They are wonderful visual reminders that Jesus, my Good Shepherd, loves me and that I need to follow right behind Him.

MY GOD DOESN'T WANT ME
To Be Afraid

Do you have a lot of fears? As women, we can struggle with a variety of fears: fear of cancer, Alzheimer's, or other health problems; fear of fire; fear of speaking in public; fear of new situations; fear that God will call our husbands or children to a place we don't want them to go; fear of being alone; fear of death; fear of the future; and on and on they go. I tend to be fearful (sheep are fearful creatures!) but have found that the more I get to know my God and allow Him to change my thinking, the less I am plagued by fears. This can be true in the lives of our children too.

When our Natalie was in elementary school, she was a very fearful child. Her vivid imagination would cause her to be especially scared at night. We talked about it, left a night-light on, prayed with her, and would occasionally even let her make a pallet on the floor by our bed, but nothing seemed to ease her fear. One day I decided to write out on 4 X 6 cards some verses about God in large letters so that she could see them by the light of her night-light. We even put some pretty stickers on them to make them special. Some of the verses were

> **Psalm 56:3–4** *What time I am afraid, I will trust in thee. In God I will praise his word, in God I have put my trust; I will not fear what flesh can do unto me.*

I Peter 5:7 *Casting all your care upon him; for he careth for you.*

Isaiah 41:10 *Fear thou not; for I am with thee: be not dismayed: for I am thy God: I will strengthen thee; yea, I will help thee; yea, I will uphold thee with the right hand of my righteousness.*

Psalm 91:4–5, 10–11 *He shall cover thee with his feathers, and under his wings shalt thou trust . . . thou shalt not be afraid for the terror by night. . . . There shall no evil befall thee, neither shall any plague come nigh thy dwelling. For he shall give his angels charge over thee, to keep thee in all thy ways.*

Sometimes in the night I would hear a sound and would check on Natalie. As I peeked in her room, I would see her going over her verse cards by the light of her little night-light. Eventually, we saw her get victory as God assured her that He loved her and was big enough to take care of her. Before she left to go to college, Natalie was cleaning out her room and found her verse cards. She brought them to me and said, "Mom, would you put these in my memory box? I don't need them anymore." Knowing her God is helping her overcome her fear. And that is where our help will lie too.

My God Wants Me
To Be Thankful and to Praise Him

Do you ever have a down day? There might not even be a good reason, but somehow you just feel a little down? Sometimes that happens to me. I remember one specific instance. Summer at a camp is a crazy time. I manage the craft shop at THE WILDS and in the summer supervise a staff of eight. At least two weeks before camp starts, everyone scrambles to make the final preparations for summer. The next week is Staff Training Week with a busy schedule of instructing and training the summer staff. Then the first two weeks of camp require a lot of energy to get things going smoothly. This particular summer, in the midst of everything else, we were planning an early August wedding. It had been five straight weeks of nonstop, morning-to-night activity—a perfect setup for wrong thinking. I was physically weary and tired of everyone asking me questions. The house was not in the best shape, and I missed my husband and my children (who were either working or away). One evening I came home to an empty house, and I was tired and lonely. I felt the tears welling up and was ready for a good "feel sorry for Mardi time."

I think all women go through times like that, especially when they're tired and stressed out. Even David experienced feeling down, as he describes in **Psalm 42:11**: "*Why art thou cast down, O my soul? and why art thou disquieted within me? hope thou in God; for I shall yet praise him, who is the health of my countenance, and my God.*"

One of the things I have been working on is responding in a godly way as soon as something comes up, even when I don't feel like it. My tendency is to react first, then think about it, and eventually go back and make it right. I want to get to where I ask, "**What do I know about my God?**" first so that my responses will be immediately right. The Holy Spirit has been working in my life in this area, and I have seen some growth. I've been trying to practice having a more thankful spirit, even when things aren't going well (according to me), because **I Thessalonians 5:18** says, "*In every thing give thanks: for this is the will of God in Christ Jesus concerning you.*"

So what did I do? Wallow and climb into "pity party pit?" No, I've been there too many times and have figured out that I don't like it there and God doesn't want me there. I grabbed my notebook and went for a walk. I turned to the section on **My God wants me to praise Him** and started going through all the things I have to praise God for. Then I went to **My God wants me to be thankful** and rehearsed all that I had to be thankful for. Another thing that really helps me when I'm down is to quote my favorite psalm,

Psalm 100

Make a joyful noise unto the Lord, all ye lands.

Serve the Lord with gladness: come before his presence with singing.

Know ye that the LORD *he is God: it is he that hath made us, and not we ourselves; we are his people, and the sheep of his pasture.*

Enter into his gates with thanksgiving, and into his courts with praise: be thankful unto him and bless his name.

For the LORD *is good; his mercy is everlasting; and his truth endureth to all generations.*

To me it captures the Christian life in a nutshell and continually points me back to God. It's a picker-upper all by itself!

So how did I do? With right thinking and focusing on God, it didn't take long to get back on track. Now, each time I feel down, I try to do the same thing. I love the Bible! It helps me.

MY GOD
Is the Judge

One of the categories that has had a huge impact on my life is **My God is the Judge**. As I mentioned earlier, God is in the process of pointing out my blind spots. The more I study Who He is, the more clearly I see myself. The idea that God is the Judge has several aspects that affect my daily life.

MY GOD IS THE JUDGE, AND I WILL ANSWER TO HIM

First is the sobering fact that my God is the Judge and I will someday stand before Him. I already have more than a hundred verses in my notebook about God's judgment or God being the Judge. It is very clear that believers will answer to God for the way they have spent their lives.

> **II Corinthians 5:10** *For we must all appear before the judgment seat of Christ; that every one may receive the things done in his body, according to that he hath done, whether it be good or bad.*

> **Galatians 6:7–8** *Be not deceived; God is not mocked: for whatsoever a man soweth, that shall he also reap. For he that soweth to his flesh shall of the flesh reap corruption; but he that soweth to the Spirit shall of the Spirit reap life everlasting.*

> **Hebrews 9:27** *And as it is appointed unto men once to die, but after this the judgment.*

I Corinthians 4:4–5 *For I know nothing by myself; yet am I not hereby justified: but He that judgeth me is the Lord. Therefore judge nothing before the time, until the Lord come, who both will bring to light the hidden things of darkness, and will make manifest the counsels of the hearts: and then shall every man have praise of God.*

My God is the Judge, and I will personally answer for the way I have lived my life and the choices I have made. Others will have to do the same. This solemn fact should cause me to evaluate my heart, my motives, my actions, and my priorities, always keeping in mind that I will someday stand before that just and holy Judge and give an account. **Romans 14:10–12** soberly reminds us that *"we shall all stand before the judgment seat of Christ. For it is written, As I live, saith the Lord, every knee shall bow to me, and every tongue shall confess to God. So then every one of us shall give account of himself to God."* We need to keep current in confessing our sin and having a clean heart before God.

I had a time in my life when I got off track in my priorities. It started out innocently. I used to love making various crafts, and to help with our limited budget, I would use them as gifts. One December a friend of ours had a selling booth at a popular craft show and asked if Ken would come to help him. He also mentioned that if I had any little crafts that I wanted to sell, I could sell them at his booth. That sounded like fun, so I whipped up a few little items and made $50. The next year I made $150, and after that, I was hooked and got my own booth. Before I knew it, crafts had become a priority and had gotten a bit out of control. At certain times of the year, I was putting them before God, my husband, and my children. The thing that really helped me (when I finally realized what I was doing) was to picture myself standing before God, the righteous Judge, and explaining to Him why crafts were so important. I was so impacted that I gave up crafts for several years (except to make a few gifts) and got my life back in order.

Knowing that God is the Judge should also motivate me to dedicate my life to helping others realize this inevitable reality since unbelievers will also answer to God. **Revelation 20:12–13** says, *"And I saw the dead, small and great, stand before God; and the books were opened: and another book was opened, which is the book of life: and the dead were judged out of those things which were written in the books, according to their works. And the sea gave up the dead which were in it; and death and hell delivered* up the dead which were in them: and they were judged every man according to their works."

MY GOD IS THE RIGHTEOUS JUDGE

A second thing I'm learning is that when someone wrongs me, it's God's job to take care of it. God is the righteous Judge: He is all-wise; He sees the whole picture; and in His time, He will take care of the problem. **Psalm 50:4, 6** says, "*He shall call to the heavens from above, and to the earth, that he may judge his people. . . . And the heavens shall declare his righteousness: for God is judge himself.*"

Have you ever been in a situation in which someone, at least from your point of view, judged you wrongly or treated you in a hurtful way? It can be very distressing. I had that happen with a friend, and it took me a long time to work through the problem biblically. Now I'm thankful for that experience because I learned so much from it, but at the time, it was devastating. I couldn't fix the situation myself and had to continually run to God with my hurt. One particular night I couldn't sleep because my mind kept rehearsing the problem. (Ken says that a woman with a problem can be like a little raccoon with an apple; the raccoon examines it from every possible angle, takes a bite out of it, dunks it in the water, and then starts the process all over again.) I finally got out of bed and asked God to give me something from His Word that would help me.

He showed me some principles in **Psalm 37:1–11** and once again pointed me back to Who He is and how that should make a difference in what I am going through. The psalm was written by David, who experienced some very difficult dealings with people in the course of his lifetime. David's first piece of advice was to "*fret not thyself.*" The word *fret* means "to glow with anger, to grow warm or burn, to be incensed or indignant." When someone hurts or wrongs us, we tend to fret. We stew over the offense and examine every angle of it. We can become indignant that anyone would treat us in this unkind manner. We even find ourselves having imaginary conversations with the person, expressing our case in eloquent and convincing language. After many years of dealing with his enemies, David warns us that fretting is not the proper or correct way to handle our distress. The rest of his advice draws our attention to some right ways of thinking, and they all involve focusing on God.

Psalm 37:3 *Trust in* **the** **L**ORD, *and do good.*

The first step in any conflict should always be for me to evaluate my own life and humbly ask God to show me where I am wrong, what I need to change, and if there is a blind spot that I am not seeing (**Matthew 7:1–5**). I should then go to the other person and attempt to resolve the problem (**Matthew 5:23–24**). Once I have done everything I possibly can to resolve the conflict biblically, if it is not a church discipline issue, I must leave it in the Judge's hands and trust Him to deal with it. My job is then to focus on trusting in the Lord and doing good instead of expending so much energy in fretting.

Psalm 37:4 *Delight thyself also in* **the** **L**ORD.

When we have ongoing problems in relationships, we find ourselves spending a great deal of our time thinking about the others involved in the situations. Thoughts about them find their way into our devotional time, our prayer time, our housekeeping time, our time with our husband or children, our driving time, our project time, our church time, and our leisure time. In my situation, I was allowing this person to dominate my thinking. I asked myself, "Who is supposed to control me?" The answer: "Only the Holy Spirit!" Instead of meditating on the hurt and how to fix it, I needed to focus my mental energy on God. Instead of fretting and stewing and "raccooning," I needed to be delighting in God. When my mind would wander to the problem, I would steer it back to God and meditate on His Word and give the problem to the righteous Judge. What an amazing difference it made!

Psalm 37:5 *Commit thy way unto* **the** **L**ORD, *trust also in him; and he shall bring it to pass.*

One important action that I can take is to diligently pray for the situation and the people involved. God can handle it! I can't. He knows the way and will make things right when He's ready. If He chooses not to, that's His business, not mine.

Psalm 37:7 *Rest in* **the** **L**ORD, *and wait patiently for him.*

God does things in His own time. I want things fixed right now, but I need to allow Him to work. His timetable is almost never the same as mine. He knows all about my problem, knows the hearts of the ones involved, and is at work whether I can see it or not. Sometimes I am allowed to see the end results, or I may never see what He has done, but that's okay. He is God, and He is the righteous Judge.

> **Psalm 37:8** *Cease from anger, and forsake wrath: fret not thyself in any wise to do evil.*

If I continue to dwell on an unresolved conflict and take things into my own hands, even if I don't believe I was at fault, I will become angry and will eventually fret myself into doing wrong. David says to put aside our hurt and anger and place ourselves in God's hands. Trust Him, delight in Him, rest in Him, wait for Him. Let Him deal with the problem. The wonderful result is found in the following verse.

> **Psalm 37:11** *But the meek shall inherit the earth; and shall delight themselves in the abundance of peace.*

If you are right with Him, God will give you a sweet peace in spite of the difficult relationship.

Knowing that God is the Judge also helped me in this situation because I had learned that He knows my heart. Even if someone misunderstands us, God is the One Who matters. Paul said in **I Corinthians 4:3–4**, "*But with me it is a very small thing that I should be judged of you, or of man's judgment: yea, I judge not mine own self . . . but he that judgeth me is the Lord.*" I want to eventually be able to think like that!

When you're going through a hurtful situation, the temptation is to want to justify yourself or protect your reputation, to teach that person a lesson, or even to get back at them in a roundabout way. But that is not our job! God says in **Romans 12:19**, "*Dearly beloved, avenge not yourselves, but rather give place unto wrath: for it is written, Vengeance is mine; I will repay, saith the Lord.*"

A word picture from teacher and counselor Jay Adams has stuck with me: "Vengeance is God's parking place. Stay out of God's parking place!" I also learned what it feels like to be judged by someone. That was good for me since I tend to do that, and this brings us to the third thing God is teaching me concerning judging.

My God Is the Judge: I Am Not

I am also learning that God doesn't want me to assume the role of the judge. I mentioned that God is working in my life in this area. The sad fact is that I judge people. I am a "black and white" person, and I often look at people and situations and make some kind of judgment. It is not that it's always a wrong judgment: it might be that they are disobeying God or making a foolish choice or decision that is against God's Word. **John 7:24** does tell us to *"judge righteous judgment,"* and **Galatians 6:1** says that *"if a man be overtaken in a fault, ye which are spiritual, restore such an one in the spirit of meekness."* I do need to be discerning, humble, and helpful when God presents the opportunity, but it is never to be with a critical, motive-reading, judgmental spirit. I sometimes get myself into trouble by thinking that I need to help people see the error of their ways and "fix" things right now. God can use me if He chooses, but the simple fact is that He doesn't need my help in the judgment department. He is the Judge, not me.

In one of my newer categories **My God doesn't want me to be judgmental**, I already have over twenty-five convicting verses. Ken has spoken on some verses in our Sunday school class that have really made an impression on me and made me think.

> **James 4:11–12** *Speak not evil one of another, brethren. He that speaketh evil of his brother, and judgeth his brother, speaketh evil of the law, and judgeth the law: but if thou judge the law, thou art not a doer of the law, but a judge. There is one lawgiver, who is able to save and to destroy: who art thou that judgest another?* [Who do I think I am to judge anyone else? That is God's job! He really doesn't need my help.]

> **Romans 14:10, 12–13** *But why dost thou judge thy brother? or why dost thou set at nought thy brother? for we shall all stand before the judgment seat of Christ. . . . So then every one of us shall give account of himself to God. Let us not therefore judge one another any more.*

> **Luke 6:36–37** *Be ye therefore merciful, as your Father also is merciful. Judge not, and ye shall not be judged: condemn not, and ye shall not be condemned: forgive, and ye shall be forgiven.*

> **Matthew 7:1–5** *Judge not, that ye be not judged. For with what judgment ye judge, ye shall be judged: and with what measure ye mete, it shall be measured to you again. And why beholdest thou the mote that is in thy brother's eye, but considerest not the beam that is in thine own eye? Or how wilt thou say to thy brother, Let me pull out the mote out of thine eye; and, behold, a beam is in thine own eye? Thou hypocrite, first cast out the beam out of thine own*

*eye: and then shalt thou see clearly to cast out the mote out of thy
brother's eye.* [If I choose to be judgmental of others, I will be
judged myself.]

I think that we can be pretty hard on people. I know I can be. Do you
have a person in your life who irritates or exasperates you because she
won't change; someone who doesn't do it the way you do; someone
who you don't think is worth fooling with; someone who's not your
type; someone you don't especially like or want to be around; someone
you have written off for one reason or another? We all do! The lesson
that God is teaching me is that instead of writing people off, deciding
that they'll never change, being angry or put out with them, or giving
up on them, He wants me to do what He does with me—patiently love
them and invest in them. We all have our problem areas, our strongholds, our struggles, and our blind spots. We want God and others to
be patient with us, but somehow we don't translate that into our relationship with the prickly people in our lives. It's not our job to judge.

One of the reasons God can be the Judge and we can't is found in
Jeremiah 9:24: *"But let him that glorieth glory in this, that he understandeth and knoweth me, that I am the LORD which exercise lovingkindness,
judgment, and righteousness, in the earth: for in these things I delight, saith
the LORD."*

God is perfect in righteousness and perfect in love, and that is why
He can be the Judge and we can't. Sometimes we think we're right,
but we don't have the love. Sometimes we have the love, and it is not
balanced with righteousness. But God always has the perfect combina-
tion, and on top of that, He knows *"the thoughts and intents of the heart"*
(Hebrews 4:12), and we really don't.

So what should I do when there are people in my life whom I don't
especially enjoy or understand? What I am learning is that I need to
love and invest and leave the judging to God. **First Peter 4:8–9** tells
us that *"above all things have fervent charity among yourselves: for charity
shall cover the multitude of sins."* That doesn't mean that we shouldn't
be discerning or that we should never confront sin because we always
need to view life through the lens of Scripture. But often we get the
cart before the horse or even sever the horse from the cart. Perhaps we
need to love first!

Ken and I are discovering that people often simply need a friend. All of us do. Love is a choice, and we can choose to love. Ken has been a good example of this to me. I fail often and have plenty of little quirks that could tend to bug people, but Ken has always "liked" me. He chooses to love all the time, and as a result, I adore him, and we have a wonderful marriage. I think this principle is a key to a good marriage or friendship. You must decide to "like" the other person and ask God to give you the love you need.

Over the years I have found that when I invest and love, God does whatever He wants to do. He might give me the opportunity to share something I've been learning in my devotions. He may open the door for a good conversation or discussion about child rearing or marriage. It could be that a kind remark that you make about another person could be used as an inspiration or gentle rebuke in your friend's life. A thoughtful deed that you do for your new friend might spur her on to do something kind for someone else. God may even allow you to be instrumental in solving a problem or conflict. When you have invested in someone and she knows you love her, God can use you in a variety of ways to be an encouragement and help. And very often, you have gained a dear and valued friend!

God has been gently showing me these principles over the last few years through His Word and a variety of situations. He wants me to leave the judging to Him and work on loving and serving others. In the next section, I will share a life-changing example of this.

My God Wants Me
To Love and Serve Others

When Jesus was spending His parting moments with His disciples, one of the themes that He mentioned several times was that they should be servants to others and that they should love one another.

> **John 13:14–15** *If I then, your Lord and Master, have washed your feet; ye also ought to wash one another's feet. For I have given you an example, that ye should do as I have done to you.*

> **John 13:34–35** *A new commandment I give unto you, That ye love one another; as I have loved you, that ye also love one another. By this shall all men know that ye are my disciples, if ye have love one to another.*

> **John 15:12–14** *This is my commandment, That ye love one another, as I have loved you. Greater love hath no man than this, that a man lay down his life for his friends. Ye are my friends, if ye do whatsoever I command you.*

Since some of Jesus' last words were to remind the disciples to love and serve others, these topics must have been of great importance to Him. In **Matthew 22:35–39**, He told us very simply what our priorities should be: *"Then one of them, which was a lawyer, asked him a question, tempting him, and saying, Master, which is the great commandment in the law? Jesus said unto him, Thou shalt love the Lord thy God with all thy heart, and with all thy soul, and with all thy mind. This is the first and great* *commandment. And the second is like unto it, Thou shalt love thy neighbour as thyself.*" Jesus gave us two commandments: love God, love others. **First John 4:8** says, "*He that loveth not knoweth not God; for God is love.*" While He was on earth, He demonstrated great love for people and always met their needs. He spent His time loving God and loving others, and that's what we should be doing with our lives too.

A good part of my married life I have been exposed to teaching on this subject. When we were newly married, Ken and I sat under the teaching of our pastor, who did a series on the "love chapter," **I Corinthians 13**. Later, when we moved, Ken chose to teach that topic in his adult Sunday school class. He would take each characteristic of love, for instance "*charity [love] suffereth long,*" and spend an entire Sunday school lesson teaching the meaning of the phrase, giving vivid word pictures, and sharing practical applications. The class was so helpful that he has repeated it every few years. In our home we memorized the **I Corinthians 13:1–8** passage and attempted to put it into practice with each other. After a while, I began to see that it was making a difference and was excited about the progress in me and in our family. Then came the test!

Ken was reared as an only child, and when his mother was diagnosed with Alzheimer's disease, we knew that the Lord wanted us to bring his parents to live with us. His father was not physically well and was unable to handle Mom by himself. Our remarkably talented and kind friends turned our basement garage into a beautiful little two-bedroom apartment, and we moved Ken's parents into it. Mom was seventy-nine years old, and Dad was seventy-eight and in poor health. Dad could have written his own medical book from experience. Included in the table of contents would have been tuberculosis, heart attack, congestive heart disease, aneurysm, stroke, leukemia, as well as open heart surgery, the loss of a thumb, the loss of an eye, and a crushed palate due to two different accidents. He always bounced back, but as you can imagine, each ailment took its toll.

Perhaps hardest of all was watching his wife's grasp of reality gradually slip away because of a disease for which there was no cure. Dad never complained but was very weak and very weary. Mom had always been a doll and was one of my favorite people. The words *sweet, kind, giving,* and *funny* described Frances Collier, and I considered her my very special friend. She enjoyed pretty things, shopping, keeping her house spotless, and playing the organ and piano. Her charming sense of humor and love of people and life made her a joy to be around.

Both Mom and Dad were saved later in life but served the Lord faithfully in their local church through music and teaching. Family was very important to them. They always spoiled us, loved their grandchildren, and helped us in so many thoughtful ways. They were nothing but good to us and were much beloved by all. Alzheimer's changed a lot of things. First of all, it changed Mom. She lost interest in her house and could no longer cook. If we left her to herself, her clothes were mismatched, dirty, or inside out. She would wander off down the street knocking on doors, asking for her deceased mother. Her sweet, passive personality became aggressive and angry. She would call people ugly names, pound on walls, and throw things. She would often cram her clothes or other belongings into a pillowcase and take them outside; she was also obsessed with "going home to Mama," who had passed away over thirty years before. We were all accused of awful things such as stealing her dishes, not telling her about her mother's death, and other worse things. Words cannot describe the sadness of losing a loved one in this way.

This new addition to our family changed our lives. Home had always been a happy place. We loved our family and enjoyed being home. I was used to my schedule, my time with my children and husband, my church activities, my job in the camp craft shop, my ministry with women, my free time, and my friends. We were busy and comfortable, and we loved our lives. Then everything changed. Suddenly we found ourselves responsible for two other people, two very sick people: their meals, their doctor's appointments, their laundry, their errands, their day, their lives.

Dad changed too. I had grown up virtually without a father since my father was hardly ever home. When Ken and I married, his dad became my "dad." We had always liked each other, and he seemed to enjoy having a daughter. Dad's personality was a little on the crusty side, but we all knew that he had a teddy bear heart underneath. He always acted as if Christmas was no big deal, but if we left out one little tradition, he was the first to object. He never wanted us to give him gifts but made sure that everyone else had a special gift envelope. Gruff ol' Dad would even write a little poetry for special occasions.

Dad and I had been close, but when they came to live with us, things changed. Because he was methodical and used to operating on his own timetable, he usually had opinions about how and when we should do things. He became grumpy and irritable and started snapping at me. This was a new experience, and it hurt my feelings and upset me.

By this time in my life, our children were all in school, and I was used to having a good bit of time to do the many things I needed to do. Meeting Mom and Dad's needs took a great deal of time, and I became frustrated because I couldn't get everything done. Between the two of them it took at least twice as long to go anywhere. I could feel the resentment creeping in because of all the extra pressure and what the situation was doing to our family. The home that had once been such a happy place was now becoming a place to be avoided. I was tormented by constant guilt because I knew I needed to spend more time with Mom and Dad, but I also needed to balance all the other things in my life. I dreaded going down to the apartment and sometimes avoided it, which in turn caused more guilt. It was a hard, hard time.

Ken was wonderful and spent hours with me, listening, discussing, making me laugh, and helping me trust God. We learned the ongoing importance of communicating with each other and our friends. We had some friends who were great, long-term encouragers who hung in there with us. Bonnie would leave loaves of fresh homemade bread on my counter with a little note reminding me that she was praying for me. Beth would call me to listen and empathize and help me with my thinking. Karen would give me medical advice and helpful books. Many others showed love in practical ways and assured us of their prayers.

At that time I had been working on my notebook for a little over two years, and it was a great source of comfort and help. I practically lived in the book of Psalms and continually went to the sections **My God is in control, My God is good, My God loves me, My God wants me to praise Him,** and others. God was showing me important truths about Himself, and I saw definite growth, but because of my selfishness, I still struggled with resentment. After about two months of misery, the Lord convicted me of my sin. I was having my devotions, and He reminded me from **I Corinthians 13:4–7** that "*charity [love] suffereth long, and is kind; [love] envieth not; [love] vaunteth not itself, is not puffed up, Doth not behave itself unseemly, seeketh not her own, is not easily provoked, thinketh no evil; Rejoiceth not in iniquity, but rejoiceth in the truth; Beareth all things, believeth all things, hopeth all things, endureth all things.*"

As I reviewed the list of the characteristics of love, I realized that I had not been practicing what I had been preaching (or what Ken had been preaching) as far as Mom and Dad were concerned. The whole passage was sobering, but I was especially convicted by "*love is not easily provoked*" and "*love suffers long and is kind.*" I repented and asked God to forgive me and give me a special love for those who were so dear to us yet so difficult to love now. I realized that only God could give me His kind of love and the ability to put it into practice—and He did.

Once again I saw change in our home, but this time positive change. As I thought about Dad, I realized that I needed to see things from his point of view. His life had been turned upside down. He had lived in the same town in Alabama all of his married life and had left behind his friends, family, and familiar surroundings; he knew that the move had upset our lives; he was sick himself; and he was watching his lifetime companion's life ebbing before his eyes.

The next time Dad fussed at me, I talked to him honestly about the situation. I told him how sad it made me and that if we were going to make it through the Alzheimer's chapter in our lives, we would have to be allies. I started making an extra effort to go down each morning to tell Dad what was on the schedule, to see if he needed anything, and to ask his opinion about the day. I tried to do special encouraging things that meant a lot to Dad such as hemming his pants and preparing things he liked to eat. We would plan our errands together and try to coordinate our schedules. Sometimes I would go down and just visit for a few minutes and share interesting things that God was doing at camp and in the lives of our children. The changes made were little changes, but done in love, they actually made a world of difference in our outlook and relationship. Even though the situation with Mom worsened, our world became stable and loving again. Dad and I were friends once more, and I actually believed that we could make it work over the long haul. We saw Dad become productive and happy again, and he even began complimenting, writing encouraging notes, helping with the camp mail, and doing thoughtful little things for us, such as offering to take us out to eat or paying for special treats. Instead of just *taking*, he started *giving* too, and what a difference it made. God performed an amazing transformation in all of us! Our God wants us to love and serve others, and His love works. "*Love never faileth*" (**I Corinthians 13:8**).

Things went along very well for about four months. It was Mom's eightieth birthday, and Dad and Mom had driven into town to buy steaks (his favorite) for the birthday celebration. As Dad was pulling out of the parking lot, he misjudged the speed of an oncoming car, and they were broadsided. My daughter Natalie, who was ten years old at the time, and I were on our way to town to buy some special decorations for Mom's birthday cake and were the first ones to come upon the scene of the accident. As we topped the hill, she screamed, "It's Grandma and Granddad's car!" and she began to cry. By God's kind providence, He allowed me to be with them until the ambulance came. They hadn't remembered to put on their seat belts, and Mom was all scrunched up on the floorboard of the front seat. She had some cuts and bruises and was very sore but was eventually all right. But Dad's poor, tired heart ruptured, and within three hours, he was in heaven.

It was not many hours before it hit me how gracious God had been to me to convict me about my lack of love and to enable me to correct it before He took Dad home. Can you imagine the deep, ongoing grief and regret that would have been mine to bear had I not learned to once again love my second dad? **Psalm 86:15** says, "*But thou, O Lord, art a God full of compassion, and gracious, longsuffering, and plenteous in mercy and truth.*" **My God is gracious and merciful.**

Often in a hard situation, a little love will turn the whole scenario around. I've seen God use His love to change hearts numerous times. No one likes to be judged or snubbed or written off, but we all appreciate genuine love. Everyone needs a friend! It's one of the things that God is slowly teaching me through knowing Him and studying the life of Jesus. Here are just a few of the verses from **My God wants me to love and serve others.**

> **Matthew 7:12** *Therefore all things whatsoever ye would that men should do to you, do ye even so to them.*

Proverbs 3:27 *Withhold not good from them to whom it is due, when it is in the power of thine hand to do it.*

Proverbs 12:25 *Heaviness in the heart of man maketh it stoop: but a good word maketh it glad.*

Romans 12:10, 13 *Be kindly affectioned one to another with brotherly love; in honour preferring one another; . . . Distributing to the necessity of saints; given to hospitality.*

Galatians 6:2, 10 *Bear ye one another's burdens, . . . As we have therefore opportunity, let us do good unto all men, especially unto them who are of the household of faith.*

Philippians 2:3b–4 *Let each esteem other better than themselves. Look not every man on his own things, but every man also on the things of others.*

My God
Is the Counselor

One of the most amazing things about this study is that I find that I am counseling myself more and more. I know that I certainly need constant help! God's Word is full of truth about God and gives the counsel I need for life. It's becoming much easier to recognize wrong thinking and apply what I know about God to solving my problems. **Psalm 119:24** points out that *"Thy testimonies also are my delight and my counsellors."* **Psalm 16:7** says, *"I will bless the LORD, who hath given me counsel."* **Proverbs 9:10** tells us that *"the fear of the LORD is the beginning of wisdom: and the knowledge of the holy is understanding."* As we grow in knowing God, He gives us wisdom and understanding about how to live.

What is fascinating about this study is that it is tailor-made for each individual: the young mother, the single woman, the college student, the business woman, the empty nester, the teacher, the mother of teens, the invalid, the child, the single mother, the pastor's wife, the counselor, the widow. As you pursue knowing God, you will find that He will meet whatever needs you have at whatever stage of life you are in. We should not be surprised at that since the Holy Spirit dwells in each born-again believer, and **Philippians 1:6** says, *"Being confident of this very thing, that he which hath begun a good work in you will perform it until the day of Jesus Christ."* What an encouragement to know that our good and loving God is at work in our lives!

Another of the interesting side effects of getting to know God and having my thinking changed has been the opportunity to help others with what they are going through. As women, we tend to struggle with some of the same types of problems, so when we see any progress in an area, quite often we are able to help someone else who might be dealing with the same difficulty. I have always shied away from counseling others because I was afraid I might not know what to say. To my astonishment, what I have been discovering is that almost every problem that people are going through can be traced to a wrong belief about God and can be helped by knowing and applying some of the truths about God to their lives. I find myself getting excited as I build friendships with others, and together we explore how some aspect of our faithful and capable God can help both of us grow.

Knowing God also helps us counsel our children with the many difficulties they face in their young lives. Doing their own personal notebook on God is a wonderful project for teens or even younger children. It will help them grow in their trust and faith in God. Our daughter started her own notebook when she was fifteen. Through the years she has added verses regularly and continues to refer to the different categories when she needs direction, help, or encouragement. The idea that the Holy Spirit tailors the study of knowing God to each individual is evident in her life. She has done in-depth studies on **My God is gracious** (about God's grace), **My God is sufficient**, and **My God is all-wise**; and they have made an obvious difference in her life.

Our son Aaron and his wife, Naomi, have had several opportunities to work with young people at camp, in their local church, and at college. It is a great privilege to counsel young people, but they have found that they must have constant answers and wisdom from God. They have used the notebook idea personally and also recommend it as a project for the students they counsel. As a couple they have learned that knowing God makes all the difference in the way they live their own lives and help others with their problems. It has thrilled me to see them face challenges with trust and dependence because of what they know and believe about God.

I often wish I had started my study when I was young. It would have altered a lot of wrong thinking in my life and enabled me to be a better mother to my children and a better wife to Ken. But I am so grateful that God has given me the privilege to learn about Him now and to share Him with others.

MY GOD
Is with Me

The thought that God is with me has always been one of my favorites because it is so comforting. Recently, the last of our four children went off to college, and the time that I had been dreading had finally arrived. As our boys grew up and left home, each left a huge hole in the house and was greatly missed. Our last one to go was our only daughter. Natalie and I had spent a lot of time together over the past few years since there was a space of almost five years between her and our third son. She and I had become very close. I had determined ahead of time that as an empty nester I would try to practice right thinking. I wanted to spend time reaching out to others instead of sitting around feeling sorry for myself.

I actually did very well during the daytime, and even nights were fine. But I must admit that there were some particular times I was dreading. The hardest times were when Ken would be away and there would be nobody else there with me at the house. I also didn't like the idea of driving home on our mountain roads after church in the dark. I have always had a busy life and have had my children with me when Ken was away, so I never spent much time thinking about what it would be like when they all left home. I don't mind being alone, and I'm not generally afraid, but there was something about the coming-home-with-no-one-in-the-house part that I dreaded.

Well, the inevitable happened. Ken had to go away for five days. During that time I was studying for a retreat with the theme of "Simple Gifts." One of my sessions was about gifts that God gives us, and one of the gifts that I had been studying was God's gift of the Holy Spirit. In Jim Berg's book *Created for His Glory* he suggests reading chapters 13 through 16 of the Gospel of John out loud and putting yourself into the scene. These important chapters contain Jesus' final instructions and words of comfort to His disciples before He went to die on the cross. As you read, you are to imagine that you are one of Jesus' disciples and He is speaking directly to you. Some of the verses in **John 14** were a special help to me. **John 14:16–17** says, "*And I will pray the Father, and he shall give you another Comforter* [Helper], *that he may abide with you for ever; Even the Spirit of truth; whom the world cannot receive, because it seeth him not, neither knoweth him: but ye know him; for he dwelleth* **with** *you, and shall be* **in** *you.*"

When it says "*He shall give you* **another** *Comforter*," several commentaries say that it means "another of the same kind." When Jesus left us to go back to heaven, He assured us that He wasn't leaving us alone. He left us another Helper, someone like Himself to be with us always. That is our comfort—He is **with** us and **in** us always. That was also my answer to my wrong thinking: I'm not alone. The Holy Spirit, God Himself, is *with* me! And He is my Helper and Comforter. He is *with* me and *in* me! I was just fine when Ken was gone that time as well as other times such as when he went on a mission trip to Africa for two and a half weeks. Of course I miss him when he's gone, and it will never be my favorite time, but I listen to sermons and God-honoring music, talk on the phone to friends or family, and stay busy taking care of responsibilities, doing projects, and trying to think of others. God has been faithful to be with me and help me, and I am learning to enjoy my time with just Him.

I always wondered how widows, singles, and single mothers manage alone. I think of missionaries in difficult cultures far from home, familiarity, and family; and I marvel at how they do it. The answer is that God is with them. He helps each of us live the Christian life and is at work in us. He promises in **Hebrews 13:5** that He will never *leave* us or *forsake* us.

This truth also comforts me concerning my children. Now that they are out of our home and on their own, it is a wonderful thought to know that God is with them. Whether they are at college, on the mission field in a third world country, or many miles away in another state, I am assured that God is with them. How consoling it is to a parent's heart to know that no matter where they are or what they are facing, God is there. Whom would I rather have with them?

The fact that God is with us was also a great consolation when Ken's mom was dying. She lived for four years after the car accident that took Dad, but she was ravaged with the effects of Alzheimer's disease. We were privileged to be with her in her dying moments and to experience the comfort of knowing that God was with her and us. This is an excerpt from a letter I wrote to family and friends right after Mom's homegoing:

> Wednesday morning was the longest, and as we sat there, Ken sought out a hymnbook (Mom was involved in church music for over 50 years), and we proceeded to sing all her old favorites and all the songs he could find about heaven. It was a sweet time, and we were greatly blessed by the meaningful words of the hymns as we watched our dear little mama gently leaving this world.
>
> We knew that our God was with us and that He was with Mom. As we quoted Scripture to her, **Psalm 23** was a great encouragement: "Yea, though I walk through the valley of the shadow of death, I will fear no evil: for thou art **with me**."
>
> The "death watch" is an emotional and memorable experience. It was a precious time, and we are grateful that the Lord allowed us the privilege to be with Mom in her final hours. To me it was a lonely time, but we knew our God was there, and He truly comforted us and gave us joy throughout the whole experience. Once again, we learned that our God is with us, and how grateful we are for that overwhelming truth.
>
> **Deuteronomy 31:8** And the LORD, he it is that doth go before thee; he will be with thee, he will not fail thee, neither forsake thee: fear not, neither be dismayed.
>
> **Isaiah 41:10** Fear thou not; for I am with thee: be not dismayed; for I am thy God: I will strengthen thee; yea, I will help thee; yea, I will uphold thee with the right hand of my righteousness.

Matthew 28:20 *Teaching them to observe all things whatsoever I have commanded you: and, lo, I am with you alway, even unto* **the end of the world. Amen.**

My God is with me . . . always!!

My God Is God

Psalm 100:3a *Know ye that the* LORD, *he is God.*

There are times in my life that in order to get my thinking back on track, I have to pull out all the stops and generally review what I know about God. I have recently found that I have a physical condition that, while not major or life threatening, will cause some limitations. To be honest, I'm not real big on limitations or changes, and I can be tempted to be discontent about getting older and not being able to do the things I'm used to doing. At times like this, I find that I have to do an overall review of what I know about God and remind myself that He is God!

Because of my need and the needs of my friends, I have put together a compilation of some helpful verses from several of my favorite categories about God in Appendix C. I call them an "emergency pack." I give them to people who are going through a trial.

When I am personally having a hard time with my wrong thinking, I give myself a good dose of God's right thinking by reviewing all these verses, and they never fail to help me. It helps me to put my little trial into perspective as I am able to view what I'm going through in light of my caring, loving, good, strong, sovereign God. He never wants to hurt me but always wants me to go through life-things for my good and His glory.

We all have needs, don't we? Sometimes we have little needs, and sometimes we have great needs. Only God can meet them. But we must know Him and go to Him because God is God!

THE END
(but Not Really)

I could keep going because God uses my notebook almost daily to teach me something about my thinking and my God. As I look back over what I have written here, I realize that some of it may seem very simple and mundane to those reading it. Lately, I have been reading inspiring books about dedicated missionaries, books about Christians who have sacrificed everything for the cause of Christ, and books about the last times and where we are headed. In comparison, what I've written about my ordinary life seems rather silly and insignificant to me. But in my heart I know that if I don't know my God in my everyday life, in the small things, when the time comes for me to face bigger trials, or even persecution for my faith, I will not be ready. I want to go through my trials in the right way, with right thinking and a right view of my God so that I can bring glory to Him. I know that the things I'm learning about God have helped me in the little, daily-living areas of my life and those same truths can be my foundation and help when the bigger trials of life come my way.

Psalm 145:1–5 expresses my heart's desire for my life: *"I will extol thee, my God, O king; and I will bless thy name for ever and ever. Every day will I bless thee; and I will praise thy name for ever and ever. Great is the LORD, and greatly to be praised; and his greatness is unsearchable. One generation shall praise thy works to another,* *and shall declare thy mighty acts. I will speak of the glorious honour of thy majesty, and of thy wondrous works."*

I don't know what you are going through in your life right now, but I know that God wants you to know Him and that your knowing Him will help you live life in a way that pleases Him. It is my heart's desire that you have been challenged to get to know God and that this will be the start of a lifelong venture, asking that penetrating question: **"What do I know about my God?"**

WHAT DO I KNOW
About My God?
SUGGESTED CATEGORIES

These are most of the categories I have in my notebook on God. I have also given you a few of my favorite verses in each category to be an encouragement and to help you get a good start.

MY GOD IS ABLE.

Daniel 3:17; Romans 4:20–21; II Corinthians 9:8; Ephesians 3:20; II Timothy 1:12; Jude 24

MY GOD IS ALL-KNOWING (OMNISCIENT).

I Kings 8:39; Job 37:16; Romans 11:33–36; Colossians 2:3; I John 3:20

MY GOD IS ALMIGHTY.

Genesis 17:1; Job 40:2; Psalm 91:1; Revelation 4:8; 15:3

MY GOD ANSWERS PRAYER.

Psalm 86:6–7; 116:1–2; 138:3; Jeremiah 33:3; I Peter 3:12

MY GOD AVENGES (VENGEANCE, REVENGE).

Deuteronomy 32:35, 42; Proverbs 20:22; Jeremiah 5:9; Romans 12:18–19; II Thessalonians 1:7–9; Hebrews 10:30–31

MY GOD IS BEAUTY.

I Chronicles 16:29; II Chronicles 20:21; Psalm 27:4; 90:17; Zechariah 9:17

MY GOD COMFORTS.

Psalm 23:4; John 14:16–18, 26–27; Romans 15:4; II Corinthians 1:3–4; II Thessalonians 2:16–17

MY GOD IS COMPASSIONATE.

Lamentations 3:21–23; Psalm 56:8–9; 86:15; Matthew 10:29–31; I Peter 5:7

MY GOD WANTS ME TO BE CONTENT.

Psalm 73:25; Matthew 6:19–21, 33; Philippians 4:11, 19; Colossians 3:1–2; Hebrews 13:5; I Timothy 6:6–8, 17–19

MY GOD IS IN CONTROL (SOVEREIGN).

I Chronicles 29:11–12; Psalm 18:30, 32; 115:3; Ecclesiastes 7:13; Isaiah 46:9–11; Acts 17:24–25, 28; Revelation 4:11

MY GOD CORRECTS (CHASTENS).

Psalm 32:3–5; Proverbs 3:11–12; Hebrews 12:5–11; Revelation 3:19

MY GOD IS COUNSELOR.

Psalm 33:11; 119:24; Proverbs 19:21; Isaiah 9:6; 46:10

MY GOD IS CREATOR.

Genesis 1:1; Psalm 100:3; Isaiah 45:11–12, 18; Acts 17:24–25; Colossians 1:16–17; Revelation 4:11

My God delivers.

Daniel 3:17, 28; Psalm 34:4, 6–7, 17–19; 50:15; Matthew 6:13; II Corinthians 1:9–10

My God wants me to be disciplined.

Proverbs 23:1–3; Romans 13:13–14; I Corinthians 9:24–27; 10:31; I Timothy 4:7–8

My God is eternal (everlasting, immortal).

Deuteronomy 33:27; I Timothy 1:17; 6:15–16; Hebrews 13:8; Revelation 1:8, 17–18

My God is faithful.

Deuteronomy 7:9; Lamentations 3:21–23; I Corinthians 10:13; I Thessalonians 5:24; I John 1:9; Revelation 19:11

My God is my Father.

Isaiah 63:16; Matthew 6:9, 26, 30–32; Romans 8:14–17; Galatians 4:4–7; Ephesians 2:18, 19; I John 3:1

My God wants me to fear Him.

Psalm 128:1–2; Proverbs 9:10; 31:30; Jeremiah 5:22; Luke 12:4–5

My God doesn't want me to be fearful.

Deuteronomy 31:6, 8; Psalm 56:3–4, 11; Isaiah 41:10; Matthew 10:28–31; John 14:27; II Timothy 1:7; I John 4:18

My God forgives.

Psalm 86:5; 103:3, 12; Ephesians 4:32; Colossians 1:14; I John 1:9

My God gives.

Psalm 68:19; John 3:16; Acts 17:24–25; II Corinthians 9:15; I Timothy 6:17; James 1:17; II Peter 1:3–4

MY GOD WANTS ME TO GIVE.

Ecclesiastes 11:1–2, 6; Luke 6:38; Acts 20:35; II Corinthians 9:6–8; Galatians 6:9–10

MY GOD IS TO BE GLORIFIED.

I Chronicles 16:24, 27–29; Psalm 24:7–10; John 1:14; I Corinthians 10:31; Revelation 5:12–13

MY GOD IS GOOD.

Psalm 34:8; 145:7–9; Nahum 1:7; John 10:11, 14; Romans 2:4

MY GOD IS GRACIOUS (GIVES GRACE).

Psalm 145:8; II Corinthians 9:8; 12:9; Ephesians 1:6–7; 2:8–9; Hebrews 4:16

MY GOD IS GREAT.

Deuteronomy 3:24; Psalm 135:5–6; Jeremiah 32:17; Luke 1:37; John 10:29; I John 4:4

MY GOD GUIDES (LEADS).

Psalm 37:5, 23; Proverbs 3:5–6; 16:9; John 10:27; 16:13; I Peter 2:21

MY GOD'S HANDS

Job 2:9–10; Psalm 139:9–10; Isaiah 64:8; John 10:28–29; Hebrews 10:31; I Peter 5:5–7

MY GOD WANTS ME TO BE HAPPY (BLESSED).

Psalm 128:1–2; Proverbs 3:13; 16:20; John 13:14–17; I Peter 4:13–14

MY GOD HATES _____ (NOT PLEASED WITH).

Numbers 11:1; Proverbs 6:16–19; Proverbs 8:13; Zechariah 8:17; Hebrews 1:9; Romans 8:7–8

MY GOD HEALS.

II Chronicles 7:14; Psalm 147:3; Isaiah 53:5; I Peter 2:24; James 5:13–16

MY GOD HEARS.

II Samuel 22:7; Psalm 34:4, 6, 15, 17; 116:1–2; 120:1; I John 5:14

MY GOD HELPS.

Psalm 46:1; 146:3, 5; Isaiah 41:10, 13; Hebrews 4:16; 13:6

MY GOD IS HOLY.

Exodus 15:11; Leviticus 19:2; Isaiah 6:3; I Peter 1:15–16; Revelation 4:8

MY GOD IS THE HOLY SPIRIT.

John 14:16–18, 26; Romans 8:14–16; I Corinthians 2:10–14; 6:19–20; Galatians 5:16–18, 22–25

MY GOD IS HOPE (GIVES HOPE).

Psalm 31:24; 42:11; Jeremiah 17:7–8; Romans 15:4, 13; Colossians 1:27

MY GOD WANTS ME TO HAVE HUMILITY.

Proverbs 16:19; Matthew 23:11–12; John 3:30; James 4:6–7, 10; I Peter 5:5–6

MY GOD IS JEALOUS.

Exodus 20:3–6; 34:14; Deuteronomy 4:23–24; Psalm 78:58; Isaiah 42:8

MY GOD GIVES JOY (GLADNESS).

Psalm 16:11; 100:1–2; John 15:9–11; Romans 15:13; Philippians 4:4

MY GOD IS THE JUDGE (JUDGMENT).

Psalm 9:4, 8; Romans 14:10–12; I Corinthians 4:2–5; II Corinthians 5:9–10; Galatians 6:7–8; Revelation 20:11–15

MY GOD DOESN'T WANT ME TO JUDGE.

Matthew 7:1–5; Luke 6:36–37; Romans 2:1–4; Romans 14:3–5, 10, 13; James 4:11–12

MY GOD IS KING.

Psalm 24:7–10; 103:19; Isaiah 6:5; I Timothy 1:17; 6:15; Revelation 19:6, 16

MY GOD KNOWS ME (MY THOUGHTS).

Job 42:2; Psalm 139:1–4, 23–24; Jeremiah 17:9–10; Hebrews 4:13

MY GOD WANTS ME TO KNOW HIM.

I Chronicles 28:9; Psalm 119:2; Jeremiah 9:23–24; James 4:8; II Peter 1:2–3; 3:18

MY GOD IS MY LIFE (GIVES LIFE).

Deuteronomy 30:20; Luke 20:38; John 10:10; 14:6; Acts 17:25, 28; Romans 14:7–8

MY GOD IS LIGHT.

Psalm 27:1; 119:105; John 1:4–9; 8:12; II Corinthians 4:4–6; I John 1:5–7

MY GOD IS LIVING.

Psalm 42:2; Jeremiah 10:10; John 14:19; Romans 6:8–11; II Timothy 1:10; Revelation 1:17–18

MY GOD LOVES _____ (DELIGHTS IN).

I Samuel 15:22; Psalm 147:10–11; Proverbs 11:20; 15:8–9; II Corinthians 9:7; Hebrews 11:6

MY GOD IS LOVE.

Jeremiah 31:3; John 3:16; Romans 5:8; 8:35, 37–39; I John 4:7–10, 19; Revelation 1:5

MY GOD WANTS ME TO LOVE AND SERVE OTHERS.

Proverbs 3:27; Matthew 22:36–39; John 13:34–35; Galatians 6:2, 9–10;
Philippians 2:3–4; I Peter 4:8–9

MY GOD IS MASTER (LORD).

Matthew 6:24, 33; Luke 6:46; John 13:13–16; Ephesians 6:5–9;
Philippians 2:9–11; Colossians 4:1

MY GOD IS MERCIFUL.

Psalm 86:13, 15; 103:8–14, 17; Micah 7:18; Luke 6:36; Ephesians
2:4–5; Titus 3:5

MY GOD'S NAME

Exodus 20:7; Psalm 148:5, 13; Proverbs 18:10; Isaiah 9:6; Matthew 6:9;
Philippians 2:9–10

MY GOD RULES THE NATIONS.

II Chronicles 20:6; Isaiah 40:15, 17; 64:2; Jeremiah 10:7, 10; Romans
13:1–3; Revelation 19:15

MY GOD WANTS ME TO BE OBEDIENT.

Deuteronomy 10:12–13; Jeremiah 7:23–24; Luke 6:46; John 14:15, 21,
24; Colossians 3:18, 20, 22; Hebrews 13:17

MY GOD IS ONE AND THREE (THE TRINITY).

Matthew 28:19; John 15:26; II Corinthians 1:21–22; 13:14; I Peter 1:2;
I John 5:6–7

MY GOD GIVES PEACE.

Isaiah 26:3–4; John 14:27; 16:33; Philippians 4:6–9; II Thessalonians
3:16; II Peter 1:2

MY GOD IS PERFECT.

Deuteronomy 32:4; Job 36:4; Psalm 18:30, 32; 19:7; Matthew 5:48;
Hebrews 5:8–9

MY GOD IS ALL-POWERFUL (OMNIPOTENT).

I Chronicles 29:11–12; Jeremiah 32:17, 27; Luke 1:37; John 10:17–18; Ephesians 1:19–20; Revelation 5:12–13

MY GOD IS TO BE PRAISED.

I Chronicles 16:8–10, 23–29; Psalm 34:1–3; 100; 150; Hebrews 13:15; Revelation 19:5-7

MY GOD WANTS ME TO PRAY.

Matthew 6:5–13; Ephesians 6:18; Philippians 4:6–7; I Thessalonians 5:17; Hebrews 4:6; James 5:13–18

MY GOD PRESERVES.

Nehemiah 9:6; Psalm 31:23; 37:28; 145:20; Proverbs 2:8; I Thessalonians 5:23

MY GOD HATES PRIDE.

Proverbs 6:16–17; 8:13; 16:5, 18–19; Daniel 4:37; James 4:6–10; I Peter 5:5–6; I John 2:15–16

MY GOD PROTECTS
(REFUGE, SAFETY, KEEPS ME, HIDES ME).

Psalm 4:8; 27:5; 91:2–15; Proverbs 18:10; John 10:28–29; Jude 24

MY GOD PROVIDES.

Psalm 23:1; 34:9–10; Matthew 6:25–34; Philippians 4:19; I Timothy 6:17; II Peter 1:3

MY GOD REWARDS OBEDIENCE AND GODLINESS.

Psalm 1:1–3; 128:1–2; Proverbs 3:1–4; I Corinthians 3:8–14; Galatians 6:7–8; Colossians 3:23–24

MY GOD IS RIGHTEOUS.

Psalm 92:15; Romans 3:21–26; 5:17–19; 9:14; I John 3:7; Revelation 16:5, 7

MY GOD WANTS ME TO BE RIGHTEOUS (GODLY).

Deuteronomy 10:12–13; Psalm 11:7; 37:3, 16–17, 23, 25, 30–31, 37; Matthew 5:6; I Timothy 6:6–12; John 3:7–10

MY GOD IS MY ROCK
(DEFENDS, FOUNDATION, FORTRESS).

Deuteronomy 32:4; II Samuel 22:2–3, 32, 47; Psalm 31:2–3; 61:2; I Corinthians 10:4

MY GOD IS THE SAVIOR (REDEEMER).

Matthew 1:21; Luke 1:77–79; I Timothy 2:3–6; Titus 3:4–7; I John 4:9–10, 14

MY GOD SEES.

Genesis 16:13; II Chronicles 16:9; Psalm 139:7, 11–12, 23–24; Proverbs 15:3; Jeremiah 16:17; Matthew 6:3–4

MY GOD WANTS ME TO BE A SERVANT LIKE JESUS.

Matthew 23:11–12; Mark 9:33–37; 10:42–45; John 13:3–5, 12–17, 34–35; Philippians 2:3–8; Colossians 3:22–24

MY GOD IS MY SHEPHERD (I AM THE SHEEP).

Psalm 23; 100:3; Isaiah 40:10–11; John 10:11, 14–16, 27–28; Hebrews 13:20; I Peter 2:25

MY GOD SPEAKS (HIS VOICE).

Genesis 1:3, 6, 9, 11, 14, 20, 24, 26; Job 37:2–6; Psalm 29:3–5, 7–9; Luke 4:32; Hebrews 1:3

MY GOD IS STRONG AND GIVES STRENGTH.

Psalm 18:1–2, 29, 32, 39; 28:7–8; Isaiah 40:28–31; Ephesians 3:16; Ephesians 6:10–17; Philippians 4:13

MY GOD IS SUFFICIENT.

Psalm 23:1; 73:25; II Corinthians 3:5; 12:9–10; Colossians 2:9–10;
II Peter 1:2–3

MY GOD IS SUPREME.

I Chronicles 29:11–14; Isaiah 43:10–11; 46:9–11; John 1:1–3;
I Corinthians 8:6; Colossians 1:15–18

MY GOD TEACHES.

Psalm 25:4–5, 8–9, 12; 119:12, 33, 66, 68; Isaiah 40:13–14; John 14:26;
Romans 15:4; Ephesians 4:20–21

MY GOD WANTS ME TO BE THANKFUL.

Psalm 100:4–5; I Corinthians 15:57; II Corinthians 9:11–15;
I Thessalonians 5:18; Ephesians 5:20; Colossians 3:15–17

MY GOD WANTS ME TO "THINK RIGHT" (TO "THINK BIBLE!").

Proverbs 16:3; Isaiah 26:3–4; Romans 12:2; II Corinthians 10:3–5;
Philippians 2:5; Philippians 4:4–9; II Timothy 1:7; James 1:5–8

MY GOD AND MY TONGUE

Psalm 139:4; Proverbs 6:16–19; 10:8–18, 31–32; 31:26; Colossians 4:6;
Ephesians 4:25–26, 29, 31–32; James 3:6–10

MY GOD WANTS ME TO TRUST HIM.

Psalm 56:3–4, 9–13; Proverbs 3:5–6; 16:20; Isaiah 26:3–4; Jeremiah
17:5–8; II Corinthians 1:9; I Timothy 6:17

MY GOD IS TRUTH.

Numbers 23:19; Deuteronomy 32:4; John 8:31–32; 14:6, 16–17; 17:3,
17; I John 5:20

MY GOD IS UNCHANGING
(IMMUTABLE, EVERLASTING, ENDURES).

Psalm 90:1–2; Isaiah 40:8; Malachi 3:6; Hebrews 1:8, 10–12; Hebrews 13:8; James 1:17

MY GOD UPLIFTS ME (HOLDS ME, SUSTAINS).

Deuteronomy 33:27; Psalm 3:3; 145:14; Isaiah 42:6; Hebrews 1:3; Jude 24

MY GOD GIVES VICTORY.

Isaiah 25:8; I Corinthians 15:54–58; II Corinthians 2:14; Philippians 4:13; I John 5:4

MY GOD IS ALL-WISE (OMNISCIENT, GIVES WISDOM).

Proverbs 2:3–6; Daniel 2:20–21; Romans 11:33–34; I Corinthians 1:18–25; Colossians 2:3; James 1:5

MY GOD WANTS ME TO BE A WITNESS.

Matthew 4:17, 19, 23; 9:37–38; 28:19–20; Acts 16:30–34; Romans 1:15–16; Colossians 4:3

MY GOD IS WITH ME (PRESENT, OMNIPRESENT).

Deuteronomy 31:6, 8; Isaiah 41:10; Matthew 28:20; John 14:16–17; Hebrews 13:5; Revelation 21:3

MY GOD IS WONDERFUL.

Job 42:2–3; Psalm 40:5; 119:129; 139:14; Isaiah 9:6; Matthew 21:14–15

MY GOD GAVE ME HIS WORD.

Psalm 19:7–11; 119 (all) 2, 9, 11, 24, 105; Isaiah 40:8; John 1:1–2; II Timothy 3:16–17; Hebrews 4:12

MY GOD WORKS IN MY LIFE.

Isaiah 64:8; Ephesians 3:20; Philippians 1:6; 2:13; I Thessalonians 2:13; Hebrews 13:20–21

MY GOD IS TO BE WORSHIPED.

Psalm 95:6–7; Job 1:20–21; John 4:21–24; Philippians 2:9–11; Revelation 7:11; 22:8–9

MY GOD IS WORTHY.

Psalm 18:3; Matthew 3:11–13; Revelation 4:11; 5:9, 11–12

MY GOD IS A GOD OF WRATH (ANGER).

Psalm 76:7–10; 90:7, 11; Jeremiah 10:10; John 3:36; Romans 1:18; Revelation 6:15–17; 14:9–11

WHAT DO I KNOW
About My God

SAMPLE OF NOTEBOOK PAGES

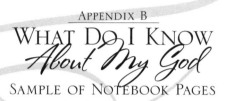

I handwrite my pages and underline the reference. They are not in any particular order—I just write them as I come across them in my Bible reading, in church, or other places. I have a lot of verses from Psalms because that's the book that I chose to go through when I started my study. This is just a sample of several pages. In my notebook this category has ten pages.

My God Is in Control

<u>Psalm 18:30</u>—As for God, his way is perfect: the word of the LORD is tried: he is a buckler to all those that trust in him.

<u>Psalm 18:32</u>—It is God that girdeth me with strength, and maketh my way perfect.

<u>Psalm 50:12</u>—If I were hungry, I would not tell thee: for the world is mine, and the fulness thereof.

<u>Revelation 19:6</u>—And I heard as it were the voice of a great multitude, and as the voice of many waters, and as the voice of mighty thunderings, saying, Alleluia: for the Lord God omnipotent reigneth.

<u>Psalm 96:10</u>—Say among the heathen that the Lord reigneth: the world also shall be established that it shall not be moved: he shall judge the people righteously.

<u>Job 23:13–14</u>—But he is in one mind, and who can turn him? and what his soul desireth, even that he doeth. For he performeth the thing that is appointed for me: and many such things are with him.

<u>Isaiah 46:9–11</u>—Remember the former things of old: for I am God, and there is none else; I am God, and there is none like me, Declaring the end from the beginning, and from ancient times the things that are not yet done, saying, my counsel shall stand, and I will do all my pleasure: Calling a ravenous bird from the east, the man that executeth my counsel from a far country: yea, I have spoken it, I will also bring it to pass; I have purposed it, I will also do it.

<u>Daniel 4:32</u> (God to Nebuchadnezzar)—And they shall drive thee from men, and thy dwelling shall be with the beasts of the field: they shall make thee to eat grass as oxen, and seven times shall pass over thee, until thou know that the most High

ruleth in the kingdom of men, and giveth it to whomsoever he will.

<u>Daniel 4:34–35</u> (Nebuchadnezzar) — And at the end of the days I Nebuchadnezzar lifted up mine eyes unto heaven, and mine understanding returned unto me, and I blessed the most High, and I praised and honoured him that liveth for ever, whose dominion is an everlasting dominion, and his kingdom is from generation to generation: And all the inhabitants of the earth are reputed as nothing: and he doeth according to his will in the army of heaven, and among the inhabitants of the earth: and none can stay his hand, or say unto him, What doest thou?

<u>Psalm 115:3</u> — But our God is in the heavens: he hath done whatsoever he hath pleased.

<u>Psalm 135:6</u> — Whatsoever the Lord pleased, that did he in heaven, and in earth, in the seas, and all deep places.

<u>Ephesians 1:11</u> — In whom also we have obtained an inheritance, being predestinated according to the purpose of him who worketh all things after the counsel of his own will.

<u>Genesis 1:1</u> — In the beginning God created the heaven and the earth.

<u>I Chronicles 29:11–12</u> — Thine, O Lord, is the greatness, and the power, and the glory, and the victory, and the majesty: for all that is in the heaven and in the earth is thine; thine is the kingdom, O Lord, and thou art exalted as head above all. Both riches and honour come of thee, and thou reignest over all; and in thine hand is power and might; and in thine hand it is to make great, and to give strength unto all.

<u>Ecclesiastes 7:13</u> — Consider the work of God: for who can make that straight, which he hath made crooked?

WHAT DO I KNOW

About My God

EMERGENCY PACK VERSES

These are some "emergency pack" verses to help you (or your friends) when you are going through a difficult time. They can also be a great encouragement for daily life. You may copy them as needed.

MY GOD CARES.

Psalm 56:8–9 *Thou tellest my wanderings: put thou my tears into thy bottle: are they not in thy book? When I cry unto thee, then shall mine enemies turn back: this I know; for God is for me.*

Lamentations 3:21–23 *This I recall to my mind, therefore have I hope. It is of the LORD'S mercies that we are not consumed, because his compassions fail not. They are new every morning: great is thy faithfulness.*

Matthew 10:29–31 *Are not two sparrows sold for a farthing? and one of them shall not fall on the ground without your Father. But the very hairs of your head are all numbered. Fear ye not therefore, ye are of more value than many sparrows.*

Hebrews 4:15–16 *For we have not an high priest which cannot be touched with the feeling of our infirmities; but was in all points tempted like as we are, yet without sin. Let us therefore come boldly unto the throne of grace, that we may obtain mercy, and find grace to help in time of need.*

I Peter 5:7 *Casting all your care upon him; for he careth for you.*

MY GOD COMFORTS.

Psalm 23:4 *Yea, though I walk through the valley of the shadow of death, I will fear no evil: for thou art with me; thy rod and thy staff they comfort me.*

John 14:16 *And I will pray the Father, and he shall give you another Comforter, that he may abide with you for ever.*

18 *I will not leave you comfortless: I will come to you.*

26 *But the Comforter, which is the Holy Ghost, whom the Father will send in my name, he shall teach you all things, and bring all things to your remembrance, whatsoever I have said unto you.*

27 *Peace I leave with you, my peace I give unto you: not as the world giveth, give I unto you. Let not your heart be troubled, neither let it be afraid.*

Romans 15:4 *For whatsoever things were written aforetime were written for our learning, that we through patience and comfort of the scriptures might have hope.*

II Corinthians 1:3–4 *Blessed be God, even the Father of our Lord Jesus Christ, the Father of mercies, and the God of all comfort; Who comforteth us in all our tribulation, that we may be able to comfort them which are in any trouble, by the comfort wherewith we ourselves are comforted of God.*

MY GOD IS IN CONTROL.

Psalm 18:30 *As for God, his way is perfect: the word of the LORD is tried: he is a buckler to all those that trust in him.*

32 *It is God that girdeth me with strength, and maketh my way perfect.*

Psalm 115:3 *But our God is in the heavens, he hath done whatsoever he hath pleased.*

Ecclesiastes 7:13 *Consider the work of God: for who can make that straight, which he hath made crooked?*

Isaiah 46:9–11 *Remember the former things of old: for I am God, and there is none else; I am God, and there is none like me, Declaring the end from the beginning, and from ancient times the things that are not yet done, saying, My counsel shall stand, and I will do all my pleasure: . . . yea, I have spoken it, I will also bring it to pass; I have purposed it, I will also do it.*

Romans 8:28–29 *And we know that all things work together for good to them that love God, to them who are the called according to his purpose. For whom he did foreknow, he also did predestinate to be conformed to the image of his Son, that he might be the firstborn among many brethren.*

Romans 11:33–34 *O the depth of the riches both of the wisdom and knowledge of God! how unsearchable are his judgments, and his ways past finding out! For who hath known the mind of the Lord? or who hath been his counsellor?*

36 For of him, and through him, and to him, are all things: to whom be glory for ever. Amen.

Revelation 4:11 *Thou art worthy, O Lord, to receive glory and honour and power: for thou hast created all things, and for thy pleasure they are and were created.*

MY GOD DOESN'T WANT ME TO BE AFRAID.

Isaiah 41:10 *Fear thou not; for I am with thee: be not dismayed; for I am thy God: I will strengthen thee; yea, I will help thee; yea, I will uphold thee with the right hand of my righteousness.*

Deuteronomy 31:6 *Be strong and of a good courage, fear not, nor be afraid of them: for the LORD thy God, he it is that doth go with thee; he will not fail thee, nor forsake thee.*

II Timothy 1:7 *For God hath not given us the spirit of fear; but of power, and of love, and of a sound mind.*

Psalm 56:3–4 *What time I am afraid, I will trust in thee. In God I will praise his word, in God I have put my trust; I will not fear what flesh can do unto me.*

Hebrews 13:5–6 *Let your conversation be without covetousness; and be content with such things as ye have: for he hath said, I will never leave thee, nor forsake thee. So that we may boldly say, The Lord is my helper, and I will not fear what man shall do unto me.*

MY GOD FORGIVES.

Psalm 86:5 *For thou, Lord, art good, and ready to forgive; and plenteous in mercy unto all them that call upon thee.*

Ephesians 4:32 *And be ye kind one to another, tenderhearted, forgiving one another, even as God for Christ's sake hath forgiven you.*

Colossians 3:12–14 *Put on therefore, as the elect of God, holy and beloved, bowels of mercies, kindness, humbleness of mind, meekness, longsuffering; forbearing one another, and forgiving one another, if any man have a quarrel against any: even as Christ forgave you, so also do ye. And above all these things put on charity, which is the bond of perfectness.*

I John 1:8–9 *If we say that we have no sin, we deceive ourselves, and the truth is not in us. If we confess our sins, he is faithful and just to forgive us our sins, and to cleanse us from all unrighteousness.*

MY GOD IS GOOD.

Psalm 31:19 *Oh how great is thy goodness, which thou hast laid up for them that fear thee; which thou hast wrought for them that trust in thee before the sons of men!*

Psalm 34:8 *O taste and see that the LORD is good: blessed is the man that trusteth in him.*

Psalm 100:5 *For the LORD is good; his mercy is everlasting; and his truth endureth to all generations.*

Nahum 1:7 *The LORD is good, a strong hold in the day of trouble; and he knoweth them that trust in him.*

John 10:11 *I am the good shepherd: the good shepherd giveth his life for the sheep.*

14 *I am the good shepherd, and know my sheep, and am known of mine.*

MY GOD GIVES GRACE (DIVINE HELP).

II Corinthians 9:8 *And God is able to make all grace abound toward you; that ye, always having all sufficiency in all things, may abound to every good work.*

II Corinthians 12:8–10 *For this thing I besought the Lord thrice, that it might depart from me. And he said unto me, My grace is sufficient for thee: for my strength is made perfect in weakness. Most gladly therefore will I rather glory in my infirmities, that the power of Christ may rest upon me. Therefore I take pleasure in infirmities, in reproaches, in necessities, in persecutions, in distresses for Christ's sake: for when I am weak, then am I strong.*

Hebrews 4:16 *Let us therefore come boldly unto the throne of grace, that we may obtain mercy, and find grace to help in time of need.*

I Peter 5:5–7 *Likewise, ye younger, submit yourselves unto the elder. Yea, all of you be subject one to another, and be clothed with humility: for God resisteth the proud, and giveth grace to the humble. Humble yourselves therefore under the mighty hand of God, that he may exalt you in due time: Casting all your care upon him; for he careth for you.*

10 But the God of all grace, who hath called us unto his eternal glory by Christ Jesus, after that ye have suffered a while, make you perfect, stablish, strengthen, settle you.

MY GOD IS HOPE.

Psalm 31:24 *Be of good courage, and he shall strengthen your heart, all ye that hope in the LORD.*

Psalm 42:11 *Why art thou cast down, O my soul? and why art thou disquieted within me? hope thou in God: for I shall yet praise him, who is the health of my countenance, and my God.*

Romans 15:4 *For whatsoever things were written aforetime were written for our learning, that we through patience and comfort of the scriptures might have hope.*

13 Now the God of hope fill you with all joy and peace in believing, that ye may abound in hope, through the power of the Holy Ghost.

MY GOD LOVES ME.

I John 4:8 . . . *for God is love.*

10 Herein is love, not that we loved God, but that he loved us, and sent his Son to be the propitiation for our sins.

19 We love him, because he first loved us.

Jeremiah 31:3 *The LORD hath appeared of old unto me, saying, Yea, I have loved thee with an everlasting love: therefore with lovingkindness have I drawn thee.*

Ephesians 2:4–5 *But God, who is rich in mercy, for his great love wherewith he loved us, even when we were dead in sins, hath quickened us together with Christ, (by grace ye are saved).*

Romans 8:35, 37–39 *Who shall separate us from the love of Christ? shall tribulation, or distress, or persecution, or famine, or nakedness, or peril, or sword? Nay, in all these things we are more than conquerors through him that loved us. For I am persuaded, that neither death, nor life, nor angels, nor principalities, nor powers, nor things present, nor things to come, Nor height, nor depth, nor any other creature, shall be able to separate us from the love of God, which is in Christ Jesus our Lord.*

MY GOD WANTS ME TO LOVE AND SERVE OTHERS.

Matthew 22:39 *And the second is like unto it, Thou shalt love thy neighbour as thyself.*

Mark 10:43–45 . . . *whosoever will be great among you, shall be your minister: And whosoever of you will be the chiefest, shall be servant of all. For even the Son of man came not to be ministered unto, but to minister, and to give his life a ransom for many.*

John 13:34–35 *A new commandment I give unto you, That ye love one another; as I have loved you, that ye also love one another. By this shall all men know that ye are my disciples, if ye have love one to another.*

Philippians 2:3–4 *Let nothing be done through strife or vainglory; but in lowliness of mind let each esteem other better than themselves. Look not every man on his own things, but every man also on the things of others.*

Galatians 6:2, 9–10 *Bear ye one another's burdens, and so fulfil the law of Christ.* . . . *And let us not be weary in well doing: for in due season we shall reap, if we faint not. As we have therefore opportunity, let us do good unto all men, especially unto them who are of the household of faith.*

MY GOD IS POWERFUL.

I Chronicles 29:11–12 *Thine, O* LORD, *is the greatness, and the power, and the glory, and the victory, and the majesty: for all that is in the heaven and in the earth is thine; thine is the kingdom, O* LORD, *and thou art exalted as head above all. Both riches and honour come of thee, and thou reignest over all; and in thine hand is power and might; and in thine hand it is to make great, and to give strength unto all.*

Jeremiah 32:17 *Ah Lord GOD! behold, thou hast made the heaven and the earth by thy great power and stretched out arm, and there is nothing too hard for thee.*

27 *Behold, I am the LORD, the God of all flesh: is there any thing too hard for me?*

Ephesians 1:19–20 *And what is the exceeding greatness of his power to us-ward who believe, according to the working of his mighty power, which he wrought in Christ, when he raised him from the dead, and set him at his own right hand in the heavenly places.*

Psalms 62:11 *God hath spoken once; twice have I heard this; that power belongeth unto God.*

Luke 1:37 *For with God nothing shall be impossible.*

MY GOD IS STRONG (GIVES STRENGTH).

Isaiah 40:28–31 *Hast thou not known? hast thou not heard, that the everlasting God, the LORD, the Creator of the ends of the earth, fainteth not, neither is weary? there is no searching of his understanding. He giveth power to the faint; and to them that have no might he increaseth strength. Even the youths shall faint and be weary, and the young men shall utterly fall: But they that wait upon the LORD shall renew their strength; they shall mount up with wings as eagles; they shall run, and not be weary; and they shall walk, and not faint.*

Ephesians 6:10–11 *Finally, my brethren, be strong in the Lord, and in the power of his might. Put on the whole armour of God, that ye may be able to stand against the wiles of the devil.*

Philippians 4:13 *I can do all things through Christ which strengtheneth me.*

II Corinthians 12:9a *And he said unto me, My grace is sufficient for thee: for my strength is made perfect in weakness.*

MY GOD WANTS ME TO "THINK BIBLE."

Isaiah 26:3–4 *Thou wilt keep him in perfect peace, whose mind is stayed on thee: because he trusteth in thee. Trust ye in the LORD for ever: for in the LORD JEHOVAH is everlasting strength.*

II Corinthians 10:3–5 *For though we walk in the flesh, we do not war after the flesh: (For the weapons of our warfare are not carnal, but mighty through God to the pulling down of strong holds;) Casting* *down imaginations, and every high thing that exalteth itself against the knowledge of God, and bringing into captivity every thought to the obedience of Christ.*

Ephesians 4:22–24 *That ye put off concerning the former conversation the old man, which is corrupt according to the deceitful lusts; And be renewed in the spirit of your mind; And that ye put on the new man, which after God is created in righteousness and true holiness.*

Philippians 2:5 *Let this mind be in you, which was also in Christ Jesus.*

Philippians 4:4–9 *Rejoice in the Lord alway: and again I say, Rejoice. Let your moderation be known unto all men. The Lord is at hand. Be careful for nothing; but in every thing by prayer and supplication with thanksgiving let your requests be made known unto God. And the peace of God, which passeth all understanding, shall keep your hearts and minds through Christ Jesus. Finally, brethren, whatsoever things are true, whatsoever things are honest, whatsoever things are just, whatsoever things are pure, whatsoever things are lovely, whatsoever things are of good report; if there be any virtue, and if there be any praise, think on these things. Those things, which ye have both learned, and received, and heard, and seen in me, do: and the God of peace shall be with you.*

James 1:5–8 *If any of you lack wisdom, let him ask of God, that giveth to all men liberally, and upbraideth not; and it shall be given him. But let him ask in faith, nothing wavering. For he that wavereth is like a wave of the sea driven with the wind and tossed. For let not that man think that he shall receive any thing of the Lord. A double minded man is unstable in all his ways.*

MY GOD WANTS ME TO TRUST HIM.

Proverbs 3:5–6 *Trust in the LORD with all thine heart; and lean not unto thine own understanding. In all thy ways acknowledge him, and he shall direct thy paths.*

Jeremiah 17:5–8 *Thus saith the LORD; Cursed be the man that trusteth in man, and maketh flesh his arm, and whose heart departeth from the LORD. For he shall be like the heath in the desert, and shall not see when good cometh; but shall inhabit the parched places in the wilderness, in a salt land and not inhabited. Blessed is the man that trusteth in the LORD, and whose hope the LORD is. For he shall be as a tree planted by the waters, and that spreadeth out her roots by* *the river, and shall not see when heat cometh, but her leaf shall be green; and shall not be careful in the year of drought, neither shall cease from yielding fruit.*

I Timothy 6:17 *Charge them that are rich in this world, that they be not highminded, nor trust in uncertain riches, but in the living God, who giveth us richly all things to enjoy.*

MY GOD IS WITH ME.

Job 36:4 . . . *he that is perfect in knowledge is with thee.*

Deuteronomy 31:8 *And the LORD, he it is that doth go before thee; he will be with thee, he will not fail thee, neither forsake thee: fear not, neither be dismayed.*

Matthew 28:20 . . . *lo, I am with you alway, even unto the end of the world.*

Psalm 46:1 *God is our refuge and strength, a very present help in trouble.*

7 The LORD of hosts is with us; the God of Jacob is our refuge.

John 14:16–17 *And I will pray the Father, and he shall give you another Comforter, that he may abide with you for ever; Even the Spirit of truth; whom the world cannot receive, because it seeth him not, neither knoweth him: but ye know him; for he dwelleth with you, and shall be in you.*